RUNNING
for a *Higher*
PURPOSE

T0204444

"As a priest I have come to understand that we cannot find time to exercise; we have to make the time. I am so excited about this book by Bishop Paprocki, who himself has made the time not only to look after his health but also to give us an understanding of the benefits of looking after our body, mind, and soul."

Fr. Rob Galea
Singer, songwriter, and author of *Breakthrough*

"Bishop Paprocki brings St. Paul's running analogies to the modern day with remarkably practical tips and stories and helps all readers evaluate whether their fitness and spiritual trajectory is pointing toward the person of Jesus as their goal and purpose."

Sr. Stephanie Baliga, F.E.
University of Illinois Cross Country (2006–2010)
Leader of Team Our Lady of Angels marathon team

"*Running for a Higher Purpose* reads like a close friend sharing a step-by-step path on how we can grow in holistic human wellness. Bishop Paprocki beautifully illuminates how experiencing God in our athletic endeavors simultaneously nurtures a healthy body and soul."

Kristin Komyatte Sheehan
Program Director
Play Like a Champion Today Educational Series

Bishop Paprocki gives us tools—based on personal experience in both realms—that will help us win the battle of assimilating our two great loves. His insights on the integration of sports and faith are relevant to athletes of every age and Christians in any sport."

Fr. Chase Hilgenbrinck
Former professional soccer player
Vocation Director for the Diocese of Peoria

RUNNING

for a *Higher*

PURPOSE

8 Steps to Spiritual and Physical Fitness

Bishop Thomas John Paprocki

AVE MARIA PRESS AVE Notre Dame, Indiana

Founded in 1865, Ave Maria Press is a ministry of the United States Province of Holy Cross.

www.avemariapress.com

Paperback: ISBN-13 978-1-64680-045-2

E-book: ISBN-13 978-1-64680-046-9

Cover image © Getty Images, Stocksy United.

Cover and text design by Christopher D. Tobin.

Printed and bound in the United States of America.

Library of Congress Cataloging-in-Publication Data

Names: Paprocki, Thomas J., author.
Title: Running for a higher purpose : 8 steps to spiritual and physical
    fitness / Bishop Thomas John Paprocki.
Description: Notre Dame, Indiana : Ave Maria Press, [2021]
Identifiers: LCCN 2020048738 (print) | LCCN 2020048739 (ebook) | ISBN
    9781646800452 (paperback) | ISBN 9781646800469 (ebook)
Subjects: LCSH: Health--Religious aspects--Christianity. |
    Running--Religious aspects--Christianity.
Classification: LCC BT732 .P37 2021 (print) | LCC BT732 (ebook) | DDC
    261.8/321--dc23
LC record available at https://lccn.loc.gov/2020048738
LC ebook record available at https://lccn.loc.gov/202004873

Contents

Introduction   vii

1. Review   1
   *We start by making an honest assessment of our situation
   and our need to improve.*

2. Reform   15
   *Once we have assessed where we need to improve, we must
   identify how to do so.*

3. Resolve   33
   *Knowing what to do will not bring about any change unless
   we resolve to put those steps into effect.*

4. Repeat   51
   *Getting started is a tough first step, but continued effort is
   needed lest we quit before seeing any real improvement.*

5. Renew   71
   *The whole point of running for a higher purpose is to bring
   about a renewal of physical and spiritual wellness.*

6. Relax   93
   *Physical exercise and spiritual exercises are both hard work, but
   effort must be balanced with rest to prevent burnout.*

7. Reward   117
   *Achieving our physical and spiritual goals brings a great
   sense of personal satisfaction and reward.*

8. Rejoice   131
    *The integration of a sound mind in a sound body leads to the
    ultimate goal of eternal happiness.*

    Epilogue   147

Introduction

I started running half a century ago and I am still running. Why? That's the question that most people ask themselves when the thought crosses their mind to take up running or someone suggests that running would be a good idea. It is also the question that we runners ask almost anytime we go out the door to run: Why am I doing this? Why should I keep on running?

This book explores some possible—and hopefully helpful—answers to those *why* questions, as well as to the *who, what, when,* and *where* questions that will naturally flow if the *why* question is answered in such a way that you are actually motivated to lace up a pair of running shoes and head for the track or trail.

The title of this book, *Running for a Higher Purpose: Eight Steps to Spiritual and Physical Fitness*, suggests first of all that running is rarely, if ever, done without a reason. We run with a goal or sense of purpose in mind. We could be running to escape an attacker who is chasing us. We may be running because we are late to catch a plane. If we are running for reasons such as these, no additional motivation is usually needed. The threat of attack and the fear of being late are themselves sufficient motivations for the adrenaline to kick in and get our feet moving quickly. Most likely, though, if we are running on a regular basis, we run as a way to stay physically fit and enhance our emotional and spiritual well-being. In this case, the driving force spurring us into action may seem more remote and less urgent, in which case we must look deeper within ourselves to find the inspiration to get moving. This book seeks to help you find your inner strength and guide you to other resources for becoming a successful runner on the path to physical and spiritual wellness.

This latter reference to spiritual wellness should tell you that this book is not just about the body mechanics of running. All athletic endeavors involve a mental focus. Yogi Berra, a Hall of Fame baseball catcher known for his witty malapropisms, which is an incorrect use of words that is nonsensical that became known as "Yogi-isms," once famously said, "Ninety percent of this game is half mental." Yogi's math might not have added up, but he certainly was making a key point that most athletes quickly recognize: the success of one's physical efforts is directly correlated to one's mental outlook.

I am not a professional athlete, but I do bring a unique perspective to athletics as a person who has served as a Catholic priest since 1978 and as a Catholic bishop since 2003. In this book, I propose that athletics also has an essential spiritual component that accompanies its physical and mental ones. Certainly, I have learned many things about spirituality from my many years of experience in ministry and as a cradle Catholic who has practiced his faith since childhood. I have also been involved in sports since childhood, playing pick-up games of floor hockey, baseball, and touch football with my six brothers and our friends from the neighborhood on the south side of Chicago. I began playing organized hockey when I was in eighth grade and took up running when I was in high school. So for me there has always been a strong connection between sports and faith, which I first set out to describe in my previous book, *Holy Goals for Body and Soul: Eight Steps to Connect Sports with God and Faith*. While that book explored this connection largely through the sport of hockey, this book focuses more on connecting the physical and spiritual aspects of running.

The goal of this book is not to make you a gold medal Olympian or a Boston Marathon winner. I have never "won" a marathon, in the sense of being the first person to cross the finish line, but I have run the full 26.2 miles in twenty-four completed marathons (as of this writing). Most people would count finishing even one marathon as a "win." The wisdom that I share in this book from my years of experience will not necessarily make you the fastest runner in the pack, but should help to make you a successful runner in the sense of someone who sets out to reach a goal and then accomplishes it by crossing the finish line.

The eight steps to physical and spiritual wellness—review, reform, resolve, repeat, renew, relax, reward, and rejoice—are intended to help you not only set goals and achieve them as a runner, but also to apply the same formula to your growing and deepening spiritual life.

Let's lace them up and begin!

1.

Review

We start by making an honest assessment of our situation and our need to improve.

Why in the world would I want to take up running? That question is a great place to start this book. Perhaps you have never run a mile or even a block in your life, but you have watched other people run and wished that you could do that too. Perhaps you are already a runner but are looking for some tips and inspiration on how to take your running to the next level. Even if you have been running for years, it is good to look back to when you started and ask what motivated you to begin in the first place.

My interest in running was sparked by the fact that three of my grandparents died in their fifties from heart disease before I was born. When I was in high school, I began to comprehend that my gene pool likely meant I was predisposed to heart disease myself unless I did something to prevent it. I began learning about the cardiovascular benefits of aerobic training by reading magazine articles and books such as Dr. Ken Cooper's *Aerobics*, and I decided that I had better take up some form of aerobic exercise if I wanted to live past my mid-fifties.

1

Jim Fixx's book *The Complete Book of Running* helped persuade me that the aerobic activity that I should take up was running. The fact that Jim Fixx died of a heart attack while jogging at fifty-two years of age just seven years after he published his book did not dissuade me. It was later learned that Fixx was genetically predisposed to heart disease, since his father had died of a heart attack at the age of forty-three after suffering a previous heart attack when he was thirty-five. Fixx's lifestyle factors before he took up running did not help: he weighed 214 pounds and smoked two packs of cigarettes per day. If anything, the reports of the factors contributing to Fixx's death only prompted me all the more to make the commitment to running at an early age if I wanted to try to overcome my own genetic predisposition to heart disease.

So when I was a senior in high school at Quigley Preparatory Seminary South on the south side of Chicago, I decided one day to go out and run a mile. We didn't have a real track, so I just did four loops around the parking lot. It felt awful. My lungs burned. My legs felt heavy. My heart was pounding. In short, I hated it. Yet I told myself that I had to try to keep doing this if I wanted to achieve my goal of physical wellness into old age. I also hoped that I would get more accustomed to running the more I ran. So began my running career.

My other motivation for running was to keep in shape to play hockey, which was and remains my favorite sport. My dad introduced me and my six brothers and two sisters to the great game of hockey when we were growing up, taking us to the Chicago Stadium to see the Chicago Blackhawks play. My brothers and I used to play floor hockey with some friends from the neighborhood in the basement below our dad's pharmacy. I began playing organized hockey when I was in eighth grade at the local Boys' Club. We played floor hockey in the gym. The first time I played there, the teams were picking sides and someone said we needed a goalie. I volunteered and loved goaltending from the start. It is a unique position with a lot of responsibility, so players tend to either like it or shun it altogether. I liked it, and thus began my hockey career!

In addition to floor hockey, I played roller hockey and eventually learned how to ice skate, but I didn't start playing ice hockey until I was about forty-five years old and joined the Masters Hockey League, an over-thirty, no-check hockey league in Chicago. I wrote more about playing hockey in my other book, *Holy Goals for Body and Soul: Eight Steps to Connect Sports with God and Faith*, but I mention it here because, as I said, a key motivation for me to start running, in addition to health reasons, was to stay in shape to play hockey.

Through college, I would run one mile a few times per week. I was chairman of the Athletic Committee at my college seminary, Niles College of Loyola University, where I was studying to become a priest. As chairman, I organized all the intramural sports, including touch football, softball, basketball, volleyball, and tennis. Naturally, I introduced floor hockey to the program. But running was still just sort of a hobby that I did in my spare time.

After college, I went to St. Mary of the Lake Seminary in Mundelein, Illinois, the major seminary for the Archdiocese of Chicago. The seminary campus at Mundelein is quite large and has a lake right in the middle of it. There is a road that goes around the lake and the distance around the lake on that road is about three miles. So I began to increase my running mileage from the one-mile runs I had been running in college to three-mile runs around the lake.

I continued to run no more than three miles at a time until my last year of seminary, when I was ordained a deacon and assigned to do my internship at St. Catherine Labouré Parish in Glenview, Illinois. There I met some high school students who ran on their cross-country team. As I began running with the team, I increased my mileage to include some six-mile runs.

Increasing My Distance and Overcoming Pain

Something rather significant happened when I increased my mileage: I began experiencing pain in my legs, particularly in my knees and shins. This is a common experience for beginning runners as they run longer distances. This kind of pain can also come to experienced and older runners, causing some to give up. I found a solution that is important to share with any runner who is experiencing this type of pain.

The father of one of the high school cross country runners was a podiatrist. When I told him I was getting pain in my knees and shins from my increased running mileage, he said I should come to his office and he would look at my feet. I replied that my feet didn't hurt; it was my legs that were causing me problems. He suggested that I come anyway, so I went to his office and he examined my feet. He told me I had fallen arches, which were causing the pain further up my legs because the biomechanical structure of the human body and all its various parts are related. A weakness in one area can cause pain further up the skeletal infrastructure. He said that my feet were as flat as pancakes and that the solution was for me to wear orthotics, that is, inserts in my shoes that would provide arch support. The podiatrist took a plaster cast of my feet and ordered the orthotics accordingly.

From the first time I started wearing the orthotics, they began working immediately. I could run longer distances with no pain in my legs. At the recommendation of my podiatrist, I began wearing the orthotics in all of my shoes, my dress shoes as well as my running shoes, and even in my ice skates. Over the years, I have had several new pairs of orthotics made. The technology has gotten more sophisticated as they can now be designed by X-ray and computer scans that provide the design specifications, rather than using a plaster cast of the feet. I am convinced that I would not have been able to run marathons or perhaps even continue running at all if it were not for my orthotics.

I have heard too many people say that they used to run but quit because they had pain in their knees or elsewhere in their legs. If running is causing you pain, I suggest that you see a podiatrist or chiropractor to check out your biomechanics. It is important, however, that your doctor have an appreciation for sports medicine, too, and not just tell you to stop running.

Considering a Marathon

After you have been running for a while, you may begin considering attempting to run a marathon. It took many years for me to even consider the idea of running a marathon. After I increased my usual running distance from one mile to three miles to six or sometimes even eight miles, that was the most I did for about twenty-five years, from 1970 to 1995. When the marathon boom began in the 1980s, people who were taking up the challenge of running a marathon and knew that I was a runner began asking me if I wanted to run a marathon. My answer was always a consistent and emphatic "No!" I would run an occasional 5K or 10K race, but the idea of running a marathon simply had no appeal to me. The distance of a marathon seemed overwhelming as did the time it would take to prepare.

Then something unexpected happened one night when my brothers and I went out for pizza after playing hockey. Remember, I have six brothers. I think five of us were together that night. It was the week between Christmas in 1994 and New Year's Day and someone asked about New Year's resolutions. We were seated at a round table and each of us took a turn going clockwise around the table telling what we had in mind for a resolution. When they got to me, I just blurted out quite spontaneously, half-jokingly, and somewhat to my own surprise, "I think I'll run a marathon next year!"

My youngest brother, Allen, was next. Right after I said I thought I would run a marathon, he said, "That's funny. I was thinking of running a marathon, too!" He was serious, and so the seed for my marathon-running career was planted!

In the next chapter, I will talk about how Allen and I went about our training for our first marathon. Before doing so, I wish to offer some reflections about how our review of our physical well-being should be a model for assessing our spiritual condition and seeing where we need to improve.

The Connection between Spiritual and Physical Wellness

If you picked up this book thinking it would help you with the physical aspects of running—such as training programs, nutrition, and what kind of shoes to wear—I will try to address such issues in the chapters that follow. If you focus only on the physical aspects, however, you will be missing a crucial element of your training program: the spiritual aspects are essential as well. Most great athletes and coaches know about this critical connection between physical success and one's emotional, psychological, mental, and spiritual state. An athlete could have all the talent in the world and superior physical ability in comparison to opponents, but if he or she is beset with emotional problems or is simply not motivated, that athlete will not succeed.

Indeed, athletes must pay close attention to the mental aspects of sports competition as well as their physical training if they hope to succeed. Another of my favorite Yogi-isms (you can tell I am a fan of Yogi Berra) is "You can observe a lot by watching." Part of your watching means paying attention to what your body and your mind are telling you.

A Sound Mind in a Sound Body

Every year *Runner's World* magazine puts out their shoe guide, which reviews various types of shoes from different brands. Some shoes are specially designed for running on a track, others for trail running, long-distance running, motion control, stability, and so on. Over the years, I have worn several different brands, including Nike, New Balance, Brooks, Saucony and Etonic running shoes, but the brand that I have been wearing the most for the past several years is ASICS. Their shoes seem to fit my foot just right and provide the arch support that my feet need. I mention ASICS not to push their product, since you should find whatever brand works best for you. But I want to talk about ASICS here in the context of the connection between the mental and physical aspects of running because of their name. The acronym ASICS stands for the Latin phrase *Anima Sana in Corpore Sano*, which translates as "a healthy soul in a healthy body," based on the saying of the Roman poet Juvenal, *mens sana in corpore sano*, which means "a sound mind in a sound body." The founder of ASICS shoes, Kihachiro Onitsuka, who started his company in 1949 in postwar Japan, adopted a company philosophy that promoted being active as an essential part of a person's overall well-being.

I have lived most of my life by that philosophy as well. I definitely feel better when I run. I have found that I think more clearly after running, which I do to start out almost every day. I am not naturally a morning person, so running in the morning helps to wake me up and get my day going. I have "written" speeches, homilies, magazine articles and chapters for books in my head while running, which I try to actually get down in writing when I get home from my run.

I have gone out running with a seemingly insoluble problem on my mind, only to have a solution come into clear focus while running. I am sure that the blood and oxygen flowing through my brain helps.

Running has also helped to keep my body sound. As I write this, I am sixty-seven years old, five feet, nine inches tall, and weigh 157 pounds, only seven pounds more than when I graduated high school fifty years ago. My blood pressure is good and my cholesterol levels are where they should be. I have already achieved my goal of living past fifty-five, so I view any additional years as icing on the cake!

In this regard, we have a significant problem with obesity in our culture. My purpose in discussing obesity is not to wade into societal debates about the "perfect" body type or size. I am only concerned with the topic of obesity as it is related to health. The only perfect size is what is healthy for you. The Center for Disease Control (CDC) and Prevention's health survey of more than 5,000 adults in 2017-2018 found that the obesity rate was 42 percent, up from the 40 percent figure that was reported in a similar study in 2015-2016. The severe obesity rate was 9 percent in the new survey, up from the 8 percent figure in the previous one. In other words, about four out of ten American adults are obese, and nearly one in ten is severely obese. By comparison, a half century ago, about one in one hundred American adults was severely obese. The obesity rate has risen about 40 percent in the last two decades.

To translate the obesity rate into pounds, a woman who is five feet four, the average height for females in the United States, is considered obese at a weight of 174 pounds and severely obese above 232 pounds. A man who is five feet nine, about the average height for males, is considered to be obese at 203 pounds and severely obese at 270 pounds.

According to Dr. William Dietz, an obesity expert at George Washington University, the findings of the CDC survey suggest that more Americans will get diabetes, heart disease, and cancer. These facts should be alarming to those who find themselves in the weight range of being obese or severely obese and should serve to spur some self-review and resolution to take steps to correct the situation.

There are many different types of fad diets touted as an easy way to lose weight. Actually, there is only one sure fire way to lose weight: burn off more calories than you take in! Of course, that is easier said than done. But running is one sure fire way to burn off more calories and, when combined with eating in moderation, is guaranteed to result in weight loss.

In terms of spiritual motivation to lose weight, the book of Genesis tells us that we are made in the image and likeness of God. If we let ourselves become overweight and obese, we disfigure the image of God in our bodies. Have you ever noticed that images of Christ hanging from the cross never depict him as being fat or obese? The Bible does not relate any athletic accomplishments of Jesus, but he was physically fit. So we too should work on keeping physically fit. We should strive to be like Jesus in body as well as in soul.

A Healthy Soul in a Healthy Body

Speaking of our souls, the measure of a healthy soul is more difficult to assess since it cannot be calculated numerically like a person's weight. Before trying to describe how to assess the health or wellness of your soul, we must first discuss what we mean by the concept of a soul.

A traditional definition of the soul is "the ultimate internal principle by which we think, feel, and will, and by which our bodies are animated. The term 'mind' usually denotes this principle as the subject of our conscious states, while 'soul' denotes the source of our vegetative activities as well" (*Catholic Encyclopedia*). Thus, the maxim "a sound mind in a sound body" would be more limited to the conscious thinking processes of one's mind, while "a healthy soul in a healthy body" would refer to the broader notion of the unconscious and unreflective aspects of a person's existence.

In the Bible, the Hebrew word *nepeŝ* is often translated as "soul." The basic meaning of this term can be best understood, it seems, in those scripture references where *nepeŝ* is translated as self or person, that is, the concrete existing self. For example, *nepeŝ* is explicitly described only in Genesis 2:7; by the reception of the breath of God into the nostrils man becomes a "living *nepeŝ*." The New Testament word for soul is the Greek *psychē*, from which we get the root of the word "psychology." The *psychē* is associated with life. It leaves the body at death (see Lk 12:20). The *psychē* as the seat of supernatural life and the object of salvation furnishes a basis for expressions such as "saving one's soul" and the "care of souls." The *psychē* or soul in the New Testament is the totality of the self which is saved for eternal life.

St. Gregory of Nyssa and St. Augustine followed the philosopher Aristotle, who understood the soul as being in union with the body. Their understanding of the human soul was as an individual spiritual substance, the "form" of the body. In other words, Christians believe that both body and soul together constitute the human unity, although the soul may be severed from the body and lead a separate existence, as happens after death. The separation is not final, however, as Christians also believe that the soul will be reunited with the body at the resurrection of all the dead at the second coming of Christ. In his *Commentary on the Soul*, St. Thomas Aquinas wrote, "A soul is that which all living things alike have in common. In this we are all alike."

In this regard, I have found in my pastoral experience that many Christians do not seem to understand the resurrection of the body as a key article of our faith. On one recent occasion when I preached a funeral homily about how we look forward to our bodies being reunited one day in a glorified form like our Lord's resurrected body, it became apparent to me by the congregation's facial expressions that people did not know or understand what I was talking about. This was more clearly expressed at the wake of a deceased child when I overheard a person seeking to console the mother by saying that that her child "was now an angel."

I understand the compassionate intent of that statement seeking to comfort a mother grieving over the loss of her child, but I thought to myself that it was theologically inaccurate. We do not become angels when we die. Angels are spiritual beings that never had a body and never will have a body. Human beings are body and soul; when we die, our bodies are separated for a time from our souls, and we continue to exist in a spiritual form only temporarily until Christ comes again and our bodies are raised up again to be reunited with our souls. That is the meaning of the article of faith in the Apostles' Creed when we say that we believe in "the resurrection of the body, and life everlasting," and similarly in the Nicene Creed when we profess that we "look forward to the resurrection of the dead and the life of the world to come." The "body" and the "dead" in these creedal statements refer to our bodies which will be raised from the dead and reunited with our souls for all eternity.

Assessing the Wellness of Our Souls

As we begin or seek to improve on a running routine, we should not only assess the condition of our bodies. We must also assess the wellness of our souls as we seek to make spiritual improvements along with physical ones. How do we assess the health and soundness of our soul? The answer is found in the Christian tradition known as the *examination of conscience*. The practice of examining one's conscience is taught by saints and mystics as a way to review our actions to see if they are in conformity with our beliefs and moral teachings, such as the Ten Commandments. Typically, an examination of conscience can be done during our evening prayer time by reviewing the events of the day, thanking God for gifts and blessings received, and asking forgiveness for our sins and transgressions. An examination of conscience is also done by Catholics before going to the Sacrament of Penance and Reconciliation, during which the penitent confesses his or her sins to a priest and receives forgiveness for these sins through the sacramental absolution of the priest.

There are several criteria by which people can examine their consciences and assess the health or soundness of their souls, such as the Ten Commandments, the Beatitudes, the seven deadly sins, the theological virtues, and the cardinal virtues. A detailed description and helpful summary of these teachings can be found in spiritual books and helpful resources such as the *Catechism of the Catholic Church*.

My main point here is that the way to begin the path to physical and spiritual wellness is to review the current state of our bodies *and* our souls by making an honest assessment of our situation and our need to improve. In the next chapter, we will consider how to reform ourselves after we have made an assessment of our bodies and souls and areas that need improvement.

Quotation

"Although I am imperfect in many ways, I wish my brethren and acquaintances to know my disposition, so that they may clearly recognize the state of my soul."
                                —The Confession of St. Patrick

Promise

I will review the current state of my body and soul to see where I need to improve.

Prayer

O God, you created us in your own image and likeness. Help us through your grace to assess our lives
with honestly and humility as the first step toward
spiritual and physical wellness, so that we may be clear
reflections of your trinitarian love. We ask this through
Christ our Lord. Amen.

2.

Reform

Once we have assessed where we need to improve, we must identify how to do so.

In chapter 1, I pointed out that the way to begin the path to physical and spiritual wellness is to review the current state of our bodies and souls by making an honest assessment of our situation and our need to improve. In this chapter, we will talk about the ways to *reform*, that is, once we have assessed where we need to improve, we must identify how to do so.

St. Paul wrote that "you should put away the old self of your former way of life, corrupted through deceitful desires, and be renewed in the spirit of your minds, and put on the new self" (Eph 4:22–24). What does it mean to "put on the new self?" This action could be associated with changing the condition of one's body or the state of one's soul, or both. In most cases, because the body and soul are so interconnected, as we saw in the previous chapter, self-improvement will necessarily involve both.

As you set out to put on the new self, it will be helpful to set some goals. In terms of goals for your body, your goals may be to lose a certain amount of weight, to fit into a smaller clothing size, to run a mile, to run a 5K or a 10K, to run a half-marathon, or indeed to run a full 26.2 mile marathon, an ultra-marathon, or more. Your goals may include some or all of these, or more.

In terms of goals for your soul, your goals may be to overcome some particular vice, such as laziness or selfishness, or to acquire some virtue, such as charity or courage, or to be more understanding and kind to others. These goals for the soul may involve taking concrete and related steps like reading the Bible more often, going to Mass every Sunday, praying more regularly, or becoming more knowledgeable and devout in your faith. Once again, your goals may include some or all of these, or more, and could be labeled with the common heading of "growing in holiness."

To be even more specific, if you are looking for spiritual goals to begin a plan to reform your life spiritually look no further than chapter 4 of St. Paul's letter to the Ephesians, directly after the direction to put on a new self. Ephesians 4:25–32 offers very specific "rules for the new life," while pointing out that change (either physical or spiritual) is not going to happen by chance or by wishful thinking. See how many rules or goals you can count in this passage:

> Therefore, putting away falsehood, speak the truth, each one to his neighbor, for we are members one of another. Be angry but do not sin; do not let the sun set on your anger, and do not leave room for the devil. The thief must no longer steal, but rather labor, doing honest work with his [own] hands, so that he may have something to share with one in need. No foul language should come out of your mouths, but only such as is good for needed edification, that it may impart grace to those who hear. And do not grieve the holy Spirit of God, with which you were sealed for the day of redemption. All bitterness, fury, anger, shouting, and reviling

must be removed from you, along with all mal-
ice. [And] be kind to one another, compassionate,
forgiving one another as God has forgiven you in
Christ.

Notice that St. Paul's rules for life are specific behaviors, not just general dispositions. All too often, morality today seems to be dumbed down into a simple platitude like promising to "be nice." There's nothing wrong with being nice, but it lacks content and specificity in terms of the ways that we should actually behave toward others in concrete situations. This is true if you want to "put on the new self" physically as well as spiritually. Be as concrete and specific as you can.

Rules for Running Well

One of the reasons I resisted running a marathon for so long is that I had a misperception of what was required in terms of training. I thought that I would have to run ten to fifteen miles per day. I was pleasantly surprised when I found out that my assumptions about marathon training were way more than I actually needed to do.

When I took the plunge after my New Year's resolution to run a marathon, my brother Allen, who made the same resolution, sent me a marathon training program by a person named Hal Higdon. I had never heard of Hal Higdon before, but I was assured that he was the guru of marathon training. I was also pleased to see that his training program seemed quite realistic and not overly demanding, relatively speaking.

Before I get into his training programs, first let me tell you a little bit about Hal Higdon. Hal began running as a student at the University of Chicago Lab School and continued running competitively at Carleton College in Minnesota, where he won several conference championships. After college, he competed in the Olympic trials and finished as high as fifth overall in the Boston Marathon. Today, Hal is a contributing editor for *Runner's World* and one of the magazine's longest-tenured writers. He achieved guru status by authoring more than three dozen books, including *Marathon: The Ultimate Training Guide* and *Hal Higdon's Half Marathon Training*. In 2003, the American Society of Journalists and Authors awarded Hal its Career Achievement Award, the highest honor given to writer members.

Most notably, Higdon offers free and paid interactive training programs and mobile apps through his website, www. HalHigdon.com. Higdon estimates that he has prepared millions of runners for the marathon, and countless more with his half-marathon, 10K, 5K, triathlon, and other programs. You can also find Hal on Facebook and Twitter, where he enjoys connecting with runners and fans from all walks of life. I met Hal when I participated in the Chicago Area Runners' Association where he was a guest speaker on several occasions. I will spend some time talking about his marathon training programs because they have successfully guided me to complete my first twenty-four marathons.

When I started training for my first marathon in the summer of 1994, Hal's program basically had three levels for marathon training: novice, intermediate and advanced. Today, he has a an even greater variety of training programs, including suggested workout schedules to prepare for running 5K, 8K, 10K, 15K, 10-mile, half-marathon, and marathon races, as well as a post-marathon program. His marathon training program also has more levels: Novice I and II, Novice Supreme, Intermediate I and II, Advanced I and II, Multiple Marathons, Boston Marathon training and even a program for senior runners who still want to run marathons, but who don't want to put in as much mileage as the programs for younger runners.

As I said earlier, before I saw Hal's schedule, I thought I would have to put in ten to fifteen miles per day for training.

In fact, the schedule for novice runners, at least in the early weeks of the program, was not that much more than I was already running. For example, the first week of the Novice I training program calls for three three-mile runs, two rest days, and a long run of six miles.

If you are a beginning runner and want some idea of what it would take for you to run a marathon, here is the schedule of Hal's eighteen-week Novice I marathon training program:

Week	Mon	Tue	Wed	Thu	Fri	Sat	Sun
1	Rest	3 mi run	3 mi run	3 mi run	Rest	6	Cross-training
2	Rest	3 mi run	3 mi run	3 mi run	Rest	7	Cross-training
3	Rest	3 mi run	4 mi run	3 mi run	Rest	5	Cross-training
4	Rest	3 mi run	4 mi run	3 mi run	Rest	9	Cross-training
5	Rest	3 mi run	5 mi run	3 mi run	Rest	10	Cross-training
6	Rest	3 mi run	5 mi run	3 mi run	Rest	7	Cross-training
7	Rest	3 mi run	6 mi run	3 mi run	Rest	12	Cross-training
8	Rest	3 mi run	6 mi run	3 mi run	Rest	Rest	**Half-marathon**
9	Rest	3 mi run	7 mi run	4 mi run	Rest	10	Cross-training
10	Rest	3 mi run	7 mi run	4 mi run	Rest	15	Cross-training
11	Rest	4 mi run	8 mi run	4 mi run	Rest	16	Cross-training
12	Rest	4 mi run	8 mi run	5 mi run	Rest	12	Cross-training
13	Rest	4 mi run	9 mi run	5 mi run	Rest	18	Cross-training
14	Rest	5 mi run	9 mi run	5 mi run	Rest	14	Cross-training
15	Rest	5 mi run	10 mi run	5 mi run	Rest	20	Cross-training
16	Rest	5 mi run	8 mi run	4 mi run	Rest	12	Cross-training
17	Rest	4 mi run	6 mi run	3 mi run	Rest	8	Cross-training
18	Rest	3 mi run	4 mi run	2 mi run	Rest	Rest	**Marathon**

One of the key features of the Hal Higdon approach, as well as most other marathon training programs, is to feature a weekly long run that gradually increases mileage over an eighteen-week period, building from six miles in the first week to twenty miles in the climactic fifteenth week. After that, you taper off for three weeks to get ready for the marathon. Notice that the weekly long runs get progressively longer, but every third week is a "step-back" week, where mileage is reduced to allow you to gather strength for the next push upward. This method has both physical and psychological benefits.

In the first week of the Novice I program, the first long run is six miles. The long run in the second week is seven miles. For a beginner, even a six-mile run may seem daunting, but after finishing it, there is a sense of accomplishment. The following week, when the schedule calls for seven miles, I said to myself that I had successfully run six miles last week. In order to do seven miles this week, I just had to go a half mile farther out on my course before turning around and heading back to the start. That did not seem too hard to do, and indeed I did it easily enough. The mileage progressed in that way, with step-back runs every three weeks to provide a respite to recover both physically and psychologically before moving on to the next increase in mileage.

The psychological benefits of the training program became apparent to me after my first twenty-mile run. Again, I had worked up to that goal gradually. After doing an eighteen-mile run and cutting back to fourteen miles the next week, I was quite pleased to finish my twenty-mile long run, which is the longest distance in the training program before actually running the 26.2-mile marathon.

What I did not expect, but what turned out to be a pleasant surprise, occurred the weekend after my twenty-mile run when the schedule called for a cutback run of twelve miles. I found myself saying to someone, "I'm only running twelve miles this week." Then I realized I had said "*only* twelve miles!" After running twenty miles, twelve miles seemed like a piece of cake. I also recalled how challenging my first six-mile run had seemed. I was indeed getting conditioned both physically and mentally.

Rules for Living Well

I volunteer as a goalie coach for our local high school hockey team. When I coach my athletes, I often tell them that I am more concerned about what is going on in their minds and souls than with their muscles. Yes, there are some things about the mechanics of goaltending that I can teach the young goalies, but if their mind is troubled and their soul is not in a good place, then their performance will be adversely affected. The same is true for anyone trying to reform his or her physical self; he or she must pay equal or more attention to the spiritual side.

Going back to the point I emphasized in the first chapter of this book, there is a strong connection between body and soul. If we want to see positive results in the achievements we hope to accomplish with our bodies, we have to make sure that our mind and soul are providing us with the proper motivation to be successful. Just as we saw that a training program contains some specific rules of behavior and goals that we must do from day to day and week to week in order to make progress, we need rules for all of our daily activities if we hope to reform our lives and achieve our goal of living well.

The most basic set of rules for living well in the Judeo-Christian tradition is the Ten Commandments. When Jesus came to earth, he taught that he was the fulfillment of the commandments. He did not come to abolish them. In fact, he summarized them with the specifications of the two great commandments: "You shall love the Lord, your God, with all your heart, with all your soul, and with all your mind. This is the greatest and the first commandment. The second is like it: You shall love your neighbor as yourself. The whole law and the prophets depend on these two commandments" (Mt 22:36–40). To improve your spiritual side, you must love God, self, and others. This admonition applies to your development as a runner too. To reform your life physically, it is wise to reform yourself spiritually with the actions of love for God, others, and yourself!

The connection between following God's commandments and being a successful runner is that our hearts are troubled when we do not follow God's will, and if our hearts are troubled, our bodies will be adversely affected and will not perform as they should. God's law is written on our hearts (see Jer 31) and we cannot escape his Laws even if we try to rationalize our misdeeds. So, for example, if we have hatred and anger in our heart or if we are involved in an illicit sexual relationship, this will have a negative impact on our psyche, which in turn will manifest itself psychosomatically in our body. If we want our body to work in harmony with our heart and mind and soul, we should follow God's commandments.

Learning from Heroes and Saints

Although running may seem to be a solitary activity, you will rely on others for their support, motivation, and, in many cases, camaraderie. Keep St. Paul's words close: "Therefore, putting away falsehood, speak the truth, each one to his neighbor, for we are members one of another" (Eph 4:25).

In fact, part of the support, motivation, and camaraderie that accompanies running comes from knowledgeable people from the running world like Hal Higdon, but also other role models that inspire us in our overall development as faithful people. Exemplary role models are often called heroes. Exemplary role models in the Church are called saints. We can make great strides in improving ourselves if we try to imitate the example of heroes and saints.

One of my great heroes is the sixteenth president of the United States, Abraham Lincoln, who guided our nation—some would say that he saved our nation—during its most difficult time, the Civil War. Lincoln had a remarkable style of leadership that became apparent just after he was elected to his first term. History reminds us that Lincoln was barely nominated by his Republican party. Going into the convention, the favorites included William H. Seward, the senator from New York, Ohio Governor Salmon P. Chase, and former Missouri Attorney General Edward Bates. But the frontrunners basically knocked each other out of the running, so the convention delegates in Chicago looked for a compromise candidate. They chose Lincoln, an up and coming Illinois politician.

In a remarkable move after winning the nomination from them and then going on to win the general election for the presidency of the United States, Lincoln took this "team of rivals" and put them in his cabinet. Seward became his Secretary of State, Chase was appointed Secretary of the Treasury, and Bates was Lincoln's Attorney General. As might be expected, Lincoln's rivals were a bit skeptical when he first asked them to join his cabinet. As time went on, they earned each other's respect and esteem, collaborating closely in governing the nation during a time of war, such that they truly mourned his loss as leader of the nation when Lincoln was assassinated. I think of this lesson in connection to running in this way: When runners gather at the start line of a race, they are all rivals in a competition. Even though running is an individual sport, for the most part, we can learn from our rivals and even help each other to be better runners. I will describe in greater detail in the next chapter how this can be done through running clubs or even just training with some running buddies.

Sports' heroes, of course, are inspiring for your running plan. I have had several sports' heroes in my lifetime. One of my first was baseball pitcher Tommy John, a man of deep faith, who was often nearly out of baseball either due to his age (he pitched past his mid-forties) or injury (he damaged the ulnar collateral ligament of his pitching elbow). The injury led his doctor, Dr. Frank Jobe, to try a new type of surgery in which a tendon from his non-pitching arm replaced the one in his pitching arm. The surgery was a success and is often used today and called "Tommy John surgery." John also faced several personal tragedies. One of his sons fell thirty-seven feet from a third floor window when he was two years old. He was in a coma for seventeen days before fully recovering. Another son died at the age of twenty-eight from a prescription drug overdose. Tommy John referenced the faithful Job from the Old Testament who was stripped of all his material and family possessions. "The Bible says that God will never put more of a burden on you than what you're able to bear," John said. "That's the basis of my faith, and what I kept coming back to in my mind. Job was like that. He was faced with everything: affliction after affliction. But he never lost his faith."

When it comes to running, the most inspiring figure in my opinion is Steve Prefontaine, known by his fans simply as "Pre." As a teenager in the late 1960s, he broke the two-mile high school record with a time of 8:41.5. Prefontaine then went to the University of Oregon, where he won the NCAA three-mile/5K all four years of his college career (1970–1973). He was also NCAA cross-country champion in 1971–1973, failing to win only in his freshman year. Fans in his native Oregon idolized him, often wearing tee-shirts proclaiming, "Go Pre." At the 1972 Olympic Trials, some of his competitors wore "Stop Pre" T-shirts while warming up!

More than simply trying to entertain his fans, Pre crafted his running skills as a means of artistic expression, as seen in this quote from him: "Some people create with words, or with music, or with a brush and paints. I like to make something beautiful when I run." Perhaps that is why he still inspires many of us.

Steve Prefontaine usually set a very fast pace at the outset of a race, trying to burn off the sprinters. At the 1972 Olympics 5,000-meter event, he ran a long, sustained increase of the pace that allowed the field to run the final 1,600 meters at four-minute mile pace, but he was ultimately outkicked in the final straightaway to lose a medal.

After the 1972 Olympics, Prefontaine was considered to be a contender for the 1976 Olympic gold at either 5,000- or 10,000-meter distances, but he never made it to games in Montreal. In late May of 1975, Pre hosted a track meet in Eugene, Oregon, to which he invited the top runners in the world, including Frank Shorter, who had won a gold medal at the 1972 Olympics in Munich. At the Eugene meet, Shorter led Prefontaine going into the last lap of the 5,000-meter race, but in the last 200 meters, Pre dug down deep as he usually did and won in 13:28.3, just 1.6 seconds short of his personal best time.

After the race, Pre attended a party with the other runners and then drove Shorter home. On his way back after dropping Shorter off, Prefontaine apparently lost control of his car, which spun high in the air, tossing him out of the car. He landed on his back and the car came crashing down on his chest. Trapped beneath the car, Prefontaine was crushed and died before the car was discovered. A toxicology report found alcohol in his blood, although the official cause of his death was registered as traumatic asphyxiation. At his death, Prefontaine was the American record holder at every distance from 2,000 meters to 10,000 meters.

Phil Knight, who co-founded Nike in 1964 with Bill Bowerman, the track coach at the University of Oregon, published an article in the June 2016 issue of *Runners World* titled "Pre and Me" in which he wrote, "Sometimes I thought the secret of Pre's appeal was his passion. He didn't care if he died crossing the finish line, so long as he crossed first. No matter what

Coach Bowerman told him, no matter what his body told him, Pre refused to slow down, ease off. He pushed himself to the brink and beyond." Personally, I keep my favorite Steve Prefontaine quote taped to my bathroom mirror to inspire me every morning. It says: "Running is not about winning, it's about guts. To give anything less than your best is to sacrifice the gift." That is a great personal philosophy, not just for running, but for life.

Putting in the Effort to Be a Saint

Spiritually, our ultimate goal is to become saints. Becoming a saint is not an impossible task. All canonized saints were sinners. Most of the stories about saints are of people who reformed their lives to follow Christ wholeheartedly. To become a saint obviously takes great effort. Developing as a runner has many parallels to the path to sainthood. It too takes hard work and discipline and yields noticeable and positive rewards. Someone may say to a person who has spent time running and training, "You look different. You look great. You are in great shape." The same words could be said to a person who has "put on Jesus Christ" (Rom 13:14) and worked toward holiness or sainthood.

There are several canonized saints we can use as our models. Many of us were given saints' names at our Baptism. We can also choose a saint's name when are confirmed. My baptismal names are Thomas and John. I asked my parents once if they had any people or saints in mind when they chose those names for me. They said no, they just liked those names (although my father's name was John, so perhaps they had that in mind, too). There are many canonized saints named Thomas, like St. Thomas Aquinas and St. Thomas Becket, and in a sense they all go back to St. Thomas the Apostle. But I eventually chose St. Thomas More and St. John Fisher as my patron saints after I obtained my law degrees in canon law and civil law, since St. Thomas More is the patron saint of lawyers. When I was named chancellor of the Archdiocese of Chicago, I looked to St. Thomas More for his patronage and intercession, since he served as Lord Chancellor of England under King Henry VIII. St. John Fisher was the bishop of Rochester, England, during that same time. They were both ordered to be beheaded by King Henry VIII when they opposed his declaring himself to be the Supreme Head of the Church of England after the pope refused to declare the invalidity of the king's marriage to Queen Catherine of Aragon so that he could marry Anne Boleyn. My Mass of Installation as bishop of Springfield in Illinois very fittingly took place on June 22, 2010, the feast day of St. Thomas More and St. John Fisher.

The name I chose for my Confirmation was Joseph. My dad's brother, Uncle Joe, was someone I looked up to as well as my dad. As St. Joseph was the foster father of Jesus, he is a great role model as a strong guardian of the family, in light of his being the strong protector of the Holy Family, Jesus and Mary.

There are also many patron saints for different professions and jobs, as well as for various causes and activities. The patron saint of athletes is St. Sebastian, who lived in the third century. Although there is no evidence that he ever played any sport, St. Sebastian is a model of extraordinary physical and spiritual strength for athletes in every sport. He joined the Roman army in AD 283, and having distinguished himself for his excellent service, was promoted to serve in the praetorian guard to protect Emperor Diocletian. When it was discovered that Sebastian was a Christian, the Emperor, who was already infamous for ordering the deaths of hundreds of Christians, ordered Sebastian to be killed by having him tied to a stake and used as target practice by archers who riddled his body with arrows, which is the way

St. Sebastian is usually depicted in pictures and holy cards. Although he amazingly survived the wounds of the arrows, the emperor ordered him to be executed a second time, this time with clubs. In a sense, it can be said that St. Sebastian was martyred twice, which is why he is looked up to for extraordinary physical strength.

St. John Paul II (1920–2005) was, in fact, a vigorous athlete, who played goalie in soccer as a youth and, later in life, even when he was pope, continued to be an avid skier and an outdoorsman who loved hiking and fishing. Shortly after he became pope in 1978, John Paul II had a swimming pool installed at his summer residence at Castel Gandolfo so he could stay fit. When some people questioned the expense, he joked that building a pool was cheaper than another conclave to elect a new pope!

Blessed Pier Giorgio Frassati (1901–1925) also loved the outdoors. He hiked, rode horses, and skied. He was also an excellent swimmer and he shared all of these activities with his friends. Blessed Pier had a great devotion of service to the poor and for the Eucharist. He died of polio, which he contracted from those he was serving.

Recently, I have started out my homilies at Masses for the Sacrament of Confirmation by asking the people in the congregation to raise their hand if they want to become a saint. The response I get is usually a lukewarm smattering of a few raised hands. So I tell them that I will put the question another way by asking how many of them want to go to heaven. Immediately all of their hands shoot up. Everyone wants to go to heaven. So I tell them that it is basically the same question: by definition, anyone and everyone in heaven is a saint, and if you want to get to heaven, you had better work on becoming a saint, through God's grace.

I can understand why people are reluctant to say they want to become saints, since the odds are against us actually being canonized a saint by the pope if he has never heard of us. But I do like to say that we should be "canonizable," that is, able to be canonized if the pope actually did hear about our lives.

Moreover, being a canonized saint is not so far off or impossible as we might think. In the summer of 2019, I met Dr. Gianna Emanuela Molla, the daughter of St. Gianna Beretta Molla, who was a physician, a working mom, a professional woman, and a loving wife. In 1961, Gianna became pregnant with her fourth child. Toward the end of her second month of pregnancy, Gianna began experiencing severe pain. Her doctors discovered she had developed a fibroma in her uterus, meaning she was carrying both a baby and a tumor. Ruling out abortion as a way to save her own life, Gianna was quite clear about her wishes, expressing to her family, "If you must decide between me and the child, do not hesitate: choose the child. I insist on it. Save the baby."

On April 21, 1962, her daughter, Gianna Emanuela Molla, was successfully delivered by Caesarean section. The doctors tried many different treatments and procedures to ensure both lives would be saved. However, on April 28, 1962, a week after the baby was born, Gianna died from a severe infection. Gianna was beatified by Pope St. John Paul II on April 24, 1994, and officially canonized as a saint on May 16, 2004. Her husband and their children, including Gianna Emanuela, attended her canonization ceremony, making this the first time a husband witnessed his wife's canonization! How cool is that?

I rode in a van with Dr. Gianna Emanuela Molla one day that summer of 2019 from the airport in Sacramento, California, to a conference at the Napa Institute. Meeting the daughter of a canonized saint brought home to me very clearly that becoming a saint is not as impossible to achieve as we may think. It was very touching to hear her talk about how she prayed every morning to her "Saint Mom" (or in Italian, *Santa Mamma*). Listening to her talk about her sainted mother, I thought of my own mother, who died in March of 2019. Mom was a saintly person, and even if she is never officially canonized a saint, I truly believe she is canonizable.

I have actually met two canonized saints: Pope St. John Paul II and St. Teresa of Calcutta. I met Pope John Paul II when I was doing my graduate studies in Rome and on several occasions after I was ordained a bishop in 2003. Each time I was in his presence, I had a clear sense that he was a saintly person, as he had a palpable aura of holiness around him. I also met St. Teresa of Calcutta when I was doing my graduate studies in Rome. I used to celebrate Mass for her community, the Missionaries of Charity, about once a month early on Saturday mornings at their convent chapel, San Gregorio, near the Colosseum. Their chapel was very simple with no pews or kneelers, and the sisters used to sit barefoot on the floor, wearing their trademark white habits and veils with the blue piping. One day as I was celebrating Mass, I noticed a small figure huddled at the back of the room near the stove. I realized it was Mother Teresa. After Mass, she came to the sacristy to thank me for celebrating the Mass. It was several years before the invention of the smart phone with a built-in camera, so unfortunately I do not have a selfie with St. Teresa of Calcutta!

Having met the daughter of a canonized saint and having met real canonized saints several times in my life, the concept of being a canonized saint is not some remote idea from centuries ago. The thought of becoming a saint is all the more appealing precisely because it is within our reach, through God's grace. The holiness of sainthood should be the ultimate goal of the reformation of our lives.

Quotation

"Sports contribute to the love of life, and teach sac-rifice, respect and responsibility, leading to the full development of every human person."

—Pope St. John Paul II

Promise

I will reform my lifestyle by identifying the ways I need to improve my spiritual and physical wellness.

Prayer

O God, you have given us our minds and bodies to be used as you intended for your honor and glory. Help us to learn from the good example of heroes and saints to follow the paths that will lead us to spiritual and physical wellness. We ask this through Christ our Lord. Amen.

3.

Resolve

Knowing what to do will not bring about any change unless we resolve to put those steps into effect.

The third step on the path to physical and spiritual wellness is *resolve*. After you review the current state of your body and your soul by making an honest assessment of your situation and your need to improve, and then develop a plan to reform your life, you must acknowledge that no change will come about unless you resolve to put those steps into effect.

Think about what happens for those who celebrate the Sacrament of Penance and Reconciliation. We reform our lives by confessing our sins to a priest, expressing contrition for having committed them, and then we receive absolution by which our sins are forgiven and we are reconciled to God. Before going into the confessional or reconciliation room, we perform an examination of conscience by which we identify the sins that we need to confess.

A key part of this process is repentance, that is, we not only express contrition for having committed these sins, but we also *resolve* not to commit them again. St. John Fisher, bishop, martyr and my patron saint, wrote, "All who have embarked on true contrition and penance for the sins they have committed, and are firmly resolved not to commit sins again for the future but to persevere constantly in that pursuit of virtues which they have now begun, all these become sharers in this holy and eternal sacrifice." In our Catholic tradition, we call that a "firm purpose of amendment," that is, we resolve to change our lives so that we do not fall into the trap of committing these sins over and over. Confessing our sins is not like going through a car wash knowing that we'll be back again the next time the car gets dirty. Although due to our weak nature we do not expect to be sinless for the rest of our lives after having received absolution of our sins. We do expect to grow in holiness by making every effort not to commit those same sins again. In the Sacrament of Penance and Reconciliation, God gives us the grace we need to turn from sin and become holy. This is also the main message of the Gospel: repent and believe in the good news of God's love and salvation (see Mk 1:15).

Just as in our spiritual lives it is pointless to examine our conscience unless we have a firm purpose of amendment to reform our lives for the better, so too in seeking physical wellness is it pointless to have reviewed where the current state of the health and fitness of our bodies is less than ideal and then not take steps to reform those shortcomings.

Strength in Numbers

After my brother Allen and I made our New Year's resolution for 1995 to run a marathon, we began our training following the Hal Higdon training program described in chapter 2. Because Allen lives in the western suburbs of Chicago and I was living at the time at Holy Name Cathedral in downtown Chicago, we were physically separate when we were training, but we were united in a spiritual sense because we were following the same training program and we would check in with each other to compare notes and see how our training was going. It helped my resolve to follow the program since I did not want to have to tell my brother that I had fallen behind him in my training. I guess sibling rivalry sometimes can help provide positive motivation too!

The summer of 1995 was especially hot, and it was difficult running by myself. As we gradually increased our weekly mileage over the course of the eighteen-week training program, we were coming up to our longest training run, a twenty-miler, three weeks before the marathon. Thankfully, Allen offered to run the twenty miles with me and we met downtown to run along the Chicago lakefront. Running together helped us to accomplish our goal. Afterward, we knew we were ready to run the full 26.2 miles.

When the day of the Chicago Marathon arrived, on October 15, 1995, Allen and I decided that we would run it together, next to each other. We lined up before the start at the signs marking the gathering area for those who wanted to run ten-minute miles. We ran together so consistently on pace the whole way that, as we approached the finish line, we heard the race announcer say over the public address system, "You have thirty seconds to finish with a ten-minute pace." As we crossed the finish line, the race photo shows my brother just a stride ahead of me, but since Allen is thirteen years younger than I am, I guess that's not bad! My official race results from the Chicago Marathon read: Finish Time 4:22:17; pace per mile 10:00.1. For someone who set out to run at a ten-minute mile pace, that's pretty darn consistent, I would say!

To put that in perspective, however, the winner of the 1995 Chicago Marathon was Eamonn Martin of the United Kingdom, who finished in 2:11:18, which meant he was running at a pace of 5:18 per mile, or about twice as face as I was running for 26.2 miles! That certainly keeps one humble, but we should not be discouraged from running marathons if we do not cross the finish line first or if others are running faster than we are or even twice as fast as we are. One of the best things about running is that we are competing against ourselves and our own physical challenges and mental weaknesses, and so I think anyone who finishes a 26.2-mile marathon should be considered a winner.

After successfully finishing my first marathon, I do remember saying out loud, "I don't ever want to do that again!" Some of my fellow runners expressed similar sentiments.

Then something unexpected happened.

After a couple of weeks of rest, having spent the previous eighteen weeks of following a daily routine of training for the marathon, I started to feel restless with pent-up energy. In fact, I would say that I missed running. So I resumed a regular running schedule of what I would call maintenance mileage of about three miles a day. I also started thinking about my marathon pace and thought, "I can run faster than that!" Before I knew it, I was already thinking about running another marathon!

Joining a Running Club and Improving My Times

Remembering how it helped when I ran my twenty-mile training run and the marathon itself with my brother at my side, I decided to join the Chicago Area Runners Association (CARA) in 1996 so I would consistently have other people to run with. Because there are so many runners in the Chicago area, CARA offers groups with a leader for the training pace you are seeking. Most clubs meet for their weekly long run early on Saturday or Sunday mornings in groups that are typically made up of between ten and fifty runners at each pace. Some paces have more runners than others as could be expected.

The first time I met with CARA for a marathon training long run on the Chicago lakefront, I joined the nine-minute per mile pace group at the intermediate mileage level. I thought taking a full minute off my average mile pace from the previous year would be a sufficient challenge to increase my speed. Much to my surprise, the nine-minute-per-mile pace felt too slow! As we were still heading north on the first leg of our training run, the 8:30 pace group had already turned around and was heading back south, so as they were running by, I just jumped over and joined the 8:30 pace group. That's the pace I trained at all summer for my second marathon. On October 20, 1996, I finished the Chicago Marathon in 3:49:44, for a pace of 8:45.7 minutes per mile. Training with a group helped me to take more than a minute per mile off my previous year's pace. There is indeed strength in numbers!

Bolstered and encouraged by that quantitative leap in speed, I decided to join the eight-minute pace group for my third Chicago Marathon in 1997. The group I joined was basically made up of a bunch of high achievers who liked to run at what felt like a sprint at a 7:45 pace. I managed to keep up with them, though.

It was sometime around the middle of that summer that I came across an article about Boston Marathon qualifying times. In case you're not aware, because of its tradition, prestige, and popularity, a person can't just sign up and participate in the Boston Marathon. There are rules for qualification. You must be at least eighteen years old and have run a sanctioned marathon in the previous year. Most importantly, you have to meet certain qualification times in marathons you have run. What caught my eye at the time was the fact that the qualifying time for a forty-five-year old male in 1997 was three hours and twenty-five minutes, which translates to a pace of 7:49 per mile. I had just celebrated my forty-fifth birthday in August and I was training at a 7:45 pace. Suddenly, the thought of qualifying for the Boston Marathon entered the realm of possibility!

Improving and Staying Humble

I did keep up my resolve training with the Boston Marathon in the back of my mind. But my pride was hurt a bit by what happened on Labor Day of 1997. After training that summer with track coach Greg Domantay, I entered the Park Forest Scenic ten-mile race. Greg was at the race to cheer on the runners he was coaching. He was standing at about the half-way mark when I passed him, and he took my picture. I was holding up five fingers on one hand and two on the other to indicate that I was running a seven-minute mile pace. Indeed my official finish time was 1:11:30, for a pace of 7:09 per mile.

Once again, however, I was kept from becoming too proud about my accomplishment. As I was approaching the finish line, I heard the public address announcer say, "We congratulate seventy-eight-year old Warren Utes on finishing in one hour and ten minutes." I thought to myself, I'm feeling great about running a ten-mile race at a seven-minute pace, and I just got beat by a seventy-eight-year old! It made such an impression on me that I remember his name to this day.

Intrigued by the story of the elderly runner who outran me, I later learned that Warren Utes took up running at the age of sixty prompted by, or more accurately, literally pushed by his daughter, Cindy James. She shared in a newspaper story that when she saw her dad spending much of his free time in front of the television, she ordered him off the couch. "He'd become so inactive, except for an occasional game of bowling, which wasn't cutting it. So one day I just pushed him out the door and told him to go run." It worked.

Utes immediately took up running in races, and in 1978, won his age group in the Park Forest Scenic ten-miler. Over the next twenty-five years, he competed in more than 270 races and almost always finished near the top of his age category. Fourteen of those races were marathons, the last of which he ran in 1998 at the age of seventy-eight in a time of 3:36:59. By the time Warren Utes died in 2017 at the age of ninety-six, he was the holder of fourteen USA Track and Field masters' records. Utes learned his lesson well from his daughter. In a profile written about him in 1995 for the *Chicago Tribune*, Utes said, "When people retire, they have to avoid that deadly triangle: sleeping, eating and watching television. You've got to keep moving." Amen to that!

Qualifying for the Boston Marathon

Inspired by runners like Warren Utes, I was even more motivated to qualify for Boston. Over the course of my marathon training that summer of 1997, there were two other runners that I usually ran with at the same pace: Bryan Gilpin and Gregg Wirtschoreck, both several years younger than me. We decided that we would *start* the 1997 Chicago Marathon together, but none of us should feel compelled to *stay* together. If someone wanted to speed up or slow down, that would be fine.

One of the things I learned in my previous two marathons was that I usually ran the marathon at or near my training pace. I also learned that I tended to slow down as the miles progressed toward the finish line. This meant that I was doing two things contrary to the advice of the marathon experts, who recommend training at a slower speed than your actual marathon pace, and running negative splits, that is, getting faster as the miles went by. My pace strategy was a modified Steve Prefontaine approach (as discussed in chapter 2): go out fast and hang on for dear life! It's a risky strategy, as going out too fast risks crashing and burning, figuratively at least!

Bryan, Gregg, and I stayed together for 13.1 miles. We were running a 7:15 pace. As we approached the half-marathon marker, Gregg announced, "I'm going to pick up the pace for the second half." Bryan and I both said, "Go for it," and Gregg took off. I knew picking up the pace at that point would not work for me.

Bryan and I stayed together for the next several miles. As we approached Chicago's Chinatown, about nineteen miles into the race, Bryan said he would pick up the pace for the last 6.2 miles after we hit the twenty-mile marker. No sooner had he said that, about a block later, he pulled up with a muscle cramp in his leg. As he stopped to work the cramp out of his leg, I stopped with him, thinking that I could use a stretch break before hitting the final 10K of the race.

Bryan worked out the cramp and we continued on. At Sox Park, home of the Chicago White Sox, about mile twenty, Bryan again pulled up with a cramp. This time, knowing I was close to my Boston Marathon qualifying time, I said, "See you later, Bryan." He wished me luck and I continued on my own.

Going another half mile, I saw Gregg walking. As I was passing him by, I yelled, "Hey, Gregg! What happened?" He yelled back, "Too fast. I crashed and burned."

It felt like the story of the tortoise and the hare from Aesop's Fables. My two younger running companions thought they would outrun their older partner, but even though I was slowing down as the miles went by, I just kept plodding along, finishing in three hours, twenty-eight minutes, and forty-five seconds, for a pace of 7:57.6 per mile.

That's not the end of the story, though. You see, in 1996 Boston Marathon race officials started to accept computer chip times for their marathon qualifying times rather than gun times. What that means is that your computer chip time is the actual time for your personal run, not the time from when the gun is shot to start the race with the elite runners. It takes most runners from a few to several minutes before they even reach the starting line at the beginning of the race. With a computer chip, your time doesn't begin until you actually go past the starting line. In 1996, however, the Chicago Marathon had not yet started using computer chips for individual runners. So I wrote to the Boston Athletic Association and told them, since I was not an elite runner in the front of the pack, and there were 14,323 total finishers at the 1997 Chicago Marathon (plus undoubtedly more at the start who didn't finish), I am sure that more than three minutes and forty-five seconds transpired between the firing of the start gun and the time when I actually crossed the start line. The Boston race officials accepted my lawyerly reasoning and wrote a letter to me saying that I had qualified for the Boston Marathon with a qualifying time of 3:25:00! In my heart, I knew that I had run even faster than that, but officially that was all I needed. Moreover, my basic strategy worked: I ran the first half of the marathon at a 7:15 pace and the second half at an 8:15 pace, averaging out to 7:45 per mile, which is what I needed for my qualifying time! The trick is to know how fast you can push yourself early in the race without crashing and burning later on. The only way to know that, of course, is with training and experience.

Running for Others

Besides running with the company and support of training partners, another way to steel your resolve to achieve your goals is to run *for* others. You can do this by choosing a favorite charity and then gathering pledges from people you know to donate money based on you completing the race. For example, if you are running a 10K, you might gather donations per kilometer. Once you have committed to some charitable cause that you will raise money for, and when people start pledging or making their donations to support your cause, this dynamic becomes a powerful incentive to carry out your plan, lest you disappoint those who have put their trust in you.

This is how it worked for me. When I was training for my first marathon, I had a lot of inner doubts about whether I would be able to finish. After all, 26.2 miles is a long way to run. I had been thinking about raising money for charity in conjunction with my run, but I hesitated in making a public commitment until I had greater certainty that I could achieve my goal. That moment came when I completed my twenty-mile training run with my brother three weeks before the Chicago Marathon.

Having successfully run twenty miles, I felt confident that I could do the additional 6.2 miles to finish. After all, 6.2 miles is only a 10K, and I had done a lot of those! So I decided to raise money for Mercy Home for Boys and Girls, where homeless and troubled youth are cared for and helped to improve their lives. I wrote a solicitation letter with a pledge form and sent it out to my family members, friends, and parishioners at Holy Name Cathedral in Chicago, where I was living at the time. In my letter, I asked donors to pledge whatever amount of money they chose, suggesting, for example, a pledge of $1.00 per mile for the 26.2 miles of the marathon, for a donation of $26.20. Almost immediately, one of the cathedral parishioners returned the pledge form to me, indicating that he was pledging $100 per mile! I thought that must have been a mistake, thinking that he really meant to give a donation of $100 total, but attached to the pledge form was a check for $2,620.00 dollars! When I saw that, I thought: I have to run the whole marathon now, because I don't want to have to give back this check for $2,620.00! Overall, the total amount of donations made to Mercy Home for Boys and Girls in support of running my first marathon was $8,901.08.

In the course of my running for charity over the years, including twenty-four marathons and two half-marathon as of this writing, I have raised over half a million dollars—$509,920.38 to be exact—for a variety of charities, including support for vocations to the priesthood and the education of our seminarians, Catholic schools, pro-life causes, Catholic Charities Mobile Food Pantry, and legal services for the poor. In fact, almost two-thirds of the total amount raised—$321,502.67—was for the Chicago Legal Clinic, a legal services program that I co-founded to help those with legal problems who could not otherwise afford to hire a private attorney. This was the main reason why I went to law school after I was ordained a priest: because I wanted to do something concrete that would help the poor, rather than talk about it.

I will admit that it is a lot easier for a priest or bishop to raise money for charity than a layperson. But if you work through your network of family members, friends, and neighbors, I am certain you can arrange for many people to pledge something for a worthy cause. My main point here is that running for charity is a great motivator and a wonderful way to strengthen your resolve to follow through on your goals, knowing that other people are counting on you to do so.

Spiritual Strength in Numbers

What I have been saying about drawing strength from numbers in our physical training also applies to drawing strength from others in our spiritual lives. Just as in physical training, if we limit our spiritual exercises to doing them alone, we run a far greater risk of becoming lukewarm in our faith, backsliding in our moral lives, tepid in our prayers, and lazy in our charitable deeds toward others.

Maintaining ties to a community of faith is especially important in our American culture, which tends to be very individualistic. Americans tend to be very independent, going about life with a "lone ranger" mentality. This carries over to the practice of religion. Some people are inclined to say, "I don't need the Church, bishop, priests, Mass, or sacraments; I can do this myself!" They also say things like, "I am spiritual, but not religious," meaning that they would rather go it alone in their faith life than seek the support of a community of faith. By "spiritual" they mean some sort of direct relationship with God that often focuses on their own inner spirit or psyche.

We see this reflected in the numbers of Catholics who go to Mass on Sundays. According to a Gallup poll conducted from 2014 to 2017, an average of 39 percent of Catholics in the United States reported attending Mass in the previous seven days. This was down from an average of 45 percent from 2005 to 2008 and represents a steep decline from 75 percent of Catholics who regularly attended Sunday Mass in 1955. While the number of Protestants who reported attending church services weekly from 2014 to 2017 was essentially unchanged from the previous decade at 45 percent, this low number was also discouraging. Taken together, this means that a majority of Christians in the United States—Catholics and Protestants—do not observe the Third Commandment's obligation to keep holy the Sabbath, which for Christians is Sunday, the day of Christ's Resurrection.

It may be of some comfort to us in the third millennium of Christianity to know that absence from the community's worship was apparently a problem for the early Church. The letter to the Hebrews contains this admonition: "We should not stay away from our assembly, as is the custom of some, but encourage one another" (10:25). Here the "assembly," or *ekklēsia* in Greek, refers to the community called together and gathered in worship. The early Christian community was keenly aware from its nascent beginning that absence from the Sunday participation in worship was discouraging to the faith of the individual members of the community, while the presence of all would help them to strengthen and encourage one another.

Religion Is Togetherness

In this regard, it is helpful to note that the word "religion" comes from the Latin word, *religare*, which means "to bind or fasten up; to bind fast." Religion binds people together and makes us far stronger spiritually as a community than we could ever be individually.

This message about not trying to go it alone was well-illustrated in the excellent documentary called the *March of the Penguins*, narrated by Morgan Freeman, about the Emperor Penguins of Antarctica. The movie tells how the Emperor Penguins make their annual walk of seventy miles from the ocean inland, which is their natural habitat, to their breeding grounds, but what is really amazing is that they make this seventy-mile journey several times back and forth to get food while nursing their eggs. Along the way, they face blizzards, ice storms, and sub-zero temperatures, which they defend against by huddling together to keep each other warm, especially the pregnant females. Unfortunately, some of the penguins, either because they are old or sickly, fall behind. Without the protection of the group, these penguins die along the way, freezing to death during the long winter, while others are killed by predators. Those penguins that fall behind eventually die because they cannot survive the winter walking alone.

A moral of the story is this: we cannot survive either if we try to walk alone through life. Human beings are social creatures, and we need each other because we draw strength from one another. Just as physically we need people to help us, spiritually we need help for our faith to survive and grow.

We saw this vividly during the coronavirus pandemic that began in earnest in 2020 with the requirements of "social distancing" and "sheltering in place." Not only was it difficult for many people suddenly to be out of work and for all of us to be unable to be with others socially, but we were even prevented from having public Masses during the most sacred time of the year, Holy Week and Easter. The most we could do was offer our liturgies for people to watch livestreamed over the internet or on television, while inviting them to make a "spiritual communion," that is, a prayer of longing or desire to be united with Christ spiritually, since people were prevented from coming to church and actually receiving Holy Communion. While it was some consolation to know that there were viewers watching at home and participating virtually, it was hard for me as a bishop and for our priests to celebrate Masses looking out at empty pews, without a congregation being physically present. I can only imagine how hard it was for parishioners not to be able to come to church and receive our Lord in the Eucharist. While social distancing was the prescription to avoid spreading a serious and, in many cases, even a lethal disease, it did not come without a spiritual and psychological cost in terms of social isolation.

I witnessed the cost of social isolation firsthand in the life of my father's older sister, my Aunt Marian Jacobs, who is also my godmother. Aunt Marian turned 102 years old on March 25, 2020! She lives in her own "independent living" apartment within a retirement community near Chicago's O'Hare International Airport. She is mentally sharp and physically doing pretty well for her age. Remember, I wrote in chapter one that I took up running because three of my grandparents died in their fifties from heart disease and I realized that my gene pool meant I needed to do regular aerobic exercise to for the sake of my cardiovascular system. Well, although my dad suffered a heart attack pretty much on schedule at the age of sixty, which he survived but which required triple-bypass surgery, his older sister is still plugging along at the age of 102 with no signs of cardiac distress. I hope I got some of Aunt Marian's genes!

Normally, I would have said my aunt *celebrated* her 102nd birthday, but in 2020 it wasn't much of a celebration. I could tell Aunt Marian was crying when I called to wish her a happy birthday. I asked her what was wrong. She said it was a very sad day. So I asked why. She said her daughter Pamela had come with her husband, along with Aunt Marian's great-granddaughter, to wish her a happy birthday, but the staff of the retirement home would not let them come through the front door because of the safety precautions put in place to help prevent the spread of the coronavirus. With my cousins standing in the foyer while my Aunt Marian was in the lobby, separated by the glass windows and doors, all they could do was wave at each other. The most I could do was assure her that I would come and celebrate with her as soon as the situation improved when visits would be permitted again. At that point, however, I worried more that my Aunt Marian would die of a broken heart rather than from the coronavirus.

Painful scenes like this played out across the world. A couple of days after my aunt's birthday, I received an e-mail from a former member of the Swiss Guard who served as a papal bodyguard during the pontificate of Pope St. John Paul II. He wrote, "The virus took my dad Alberto in just three days. My parents live in northern Italy. I'm an only child. My poor mom can't go out and nobody could go in with my dad. They took his body and told my mom they will bring her some ashes in a month or so. Awful!"

Yes, this was an awful situation. As we all try to cope as best we can under difficult circumstances, it is crucial that we not forget the role that our faith can and must have in the midst of a crisis such as this. While attention rightfully focuses on the advice of health care experts and the decisions that government officials must make to protect public health and safety, we must at the same time keep God front and center in our awareness and maintain a vigorous life of prayer, trusting in God's providence to deliver us from evil and affliction. Perhaps it is fitting that this scourge descended upon us during Lent, a time of offering prayers, almsgiving, penance and fasting in atonement for our sins.

Jesus founded the Church on the Rock of St. Peter, saying, "Upon this rock I will build my Church" (Mt 16:18). Jesus was not talking about a church building, but about building a community of faith. Nor did Jesus come to teach some sort of personal philosophy of life, like the one constructed by the Chinese philosopher Confucius. Jesus came as our Redeemer to gather people into the family of God as beloved sons and daughters of the Father. The good news for us is that we don't have to walk alone on our journey of faith. The whole Church is there to walk with us.

Quotation

"Resolve to perform what you ought; perform without fail what you resolve."

—Benjamin Franklin

Promise

I will resolve to put into effect the steps that will help me to achieve my goals.

Prayer

O God, time and again you have shown your love for your people despite our sins and weaknesses. You have given us the Church to strengthen our resolve to put our faith into practice. Help us to be steadfast in our love for you and give us the grace to love our neighbors as ourselves. We ask this through Christ our Lord. Amen.

4.

Repeat

Getting started is a tough first step, but continued effort is needed lest we quit before seeing any real improvement.

In chapter 3, we addressed the importance of having a resolve to put into practice any steps we have promised ourselves for getting in shape physically and spiritually. We discussed some ways to help strengthen our resolve, such as by joining a group or running for charity. Even with this kind of help, we can slip in our progress. In this chapter, we will look at how repeated effort is needed lest we quit before seeing any real improvement. Because once is not good enough.

Repeated effort came into focus for me when I realized that qualifying for the Boston Marathon was within reach. I decided to start doing speed workouts with a coach, Greg Domantay, at Chicago's Lake Shore Park across the street from Northwestern Law School. That was convenient for me because I was living just a few blocks away at Holy Name Cathedral. We used to meet on Wednesday mornings for a one-hour speed workout. Greg called his program "Run Chicago" and his motto was "Make Things Happen."

Greg made things happen for us every Wednesday by having us repeat running various segments that always totaled three miles. For example, we might run four three-fourth mile segments one week and then six half-mile segments the next. Some weeks we would run three one-milers. There were even repeats of smaller quarter-mile segments, totaling twelve. There were always timed intervals between segments so that we could catch our breath and get a swig of water. Before doing these repeats, we always did a couple of warm-up laps, and after the speed workout we did a couple of cool-down laps. I would always run the half mile from home at the cathedral rectory to the track and then run back home after the workout. So my total mileage on my track workout Wednesdays was five miles.

An obvious physical benefit of doing these repeat segments was to train our fast-twitch muscles to help us run faster on the weekend long runs. Twitch muscles help support movement. Fast-twitch muscles help with sudden bursts of energy like jumping and sprinting. There was also a psychological benefit to doing repeat segments in that the slower pace of the long runs always felt more comfortable after having pushed to run all-out as fast as possible at the previous week's speed workout.

The whole point of repeating the same exercises is that repeated activity helps to improve the condition of your body *and* your soul. It would be just as ludicrous to say, "I just ran a quarter mile, so why do I have to run eleven more quarter-mile repeats," as it would be to ask, "I just ran yesterday, so why do I have to run again today?" The answer, we know, is that repetition is how we improve.

The same is true spiritually. We would never say, "I prayed yesterday, so why do I have to pray today?" Nor should we ever say, "I went to church last Sunday, so why do I have to go to church again this Sunday, or indeed, every Sunday?" The answer is that just as running repeat segments improves the condition of our bodies, repeating our prayers on a regular basis will improve the condition of our souls.

Repeating My "Birthday Mile"

As a newly ordained priest in 1978, I served as associate pastor at St. Michael Church in South Chicago, located at 8237 South Shore Drive. An address on South Shore Drive sounds like luxurious living, and our parish church was indeed a beautiful Gothic structure. But don't imagine my location as exactly being a lush waterfront resort, because there was a steel mill between the parish property and Lake Michigan! When I looked outside my bedroom window at night, I would see the orange glow from the blast furnaces of the South Works of United States Steel, which at the time employed 8,500 people. Most of our parishioners worked there or at the other steel mills in the area, Wisconsin Steel and Republic Steel.

During the eight years that I served in South Chicago (at St. Michael parish for five years and then as parochial administrator at nearby St. Joseph parish for three years), those steel mills gradually shut down and eventually closed as American steel production was being moved from the United States to foreign countries where labor was less expensive. Unemployment soared to 35 percent around South Chicago. It was this experience of serving the poor that motivated me to enroll at DePaul University College of Law and to study for a degree in civil law. When I graduated and passed the Illinois bar exam, I co-founded the Chicago Legal Clinic to provide legal services for the poor and unemployed, like many people in my parishes.

I am giving you this background information about me for three insights connected to running.

First, the discipline of running helped me to pursue the very demanding schedule I had to keep in order to achieve my goals. As a full-time parish priest also attending law school full-time, my days were rigorous and full. Most weekday mornings would start with Mass at 6:30, followed by a quick breakfast, and then off to downtown Chicago for a class that began at eight. After a full day of studying the usual law school curriculum of contracts, torts, civil procedure, property, taxation, and more, I would get home around four and try to get in a quick run before dinner with the other two parish priests. I would usually have appointments with parishioners until about 8:30. It was only then that I could begin my law school studies. I would usually be up until at least midnight. The next day, I repeated the same routine and did so for three years until I finished law school.

Some days I would run early in the morning instead of in the afternoon. I also did longer runs on the weekends at Calumet Park, on the lakefront south of the steel plant. My point is that even with such a demanding schedule, I made time for running. But perhaps it would be more accurate to say that *because* I made time for running, I was able to keep such a demanding schedule. I found over the years that runners typically tend to be goal-oriented people with careers that demand discipline and dedication, in fields such as law, medicine, business, or religious life. I don't think it is just that goal-oriented people like us seek out goal-oriented activities like running marathons, but rather than it is precisely by running that we acquire the physical and mental fitness necessary to live a lifestyle that is rigorous and demanding,

A second insight I had about running actually came during my first year as a priest. On Christmas Eve in 1978 I went out for a run a few hours before midnight Mass. I should let you know that I run outside even in the cold of winter. As it gets colder I just add more layers of clothing. Also, once you get moving, your body generates heat to keep you warm. In fact, I often find myself taking off my gloves after a mile or two of running in the cold because my hands get too warm.

I far prefer layering up and running outside in the cold than running indoors on a treadmill, which seems so monotonous and boring to me. I like to run outside where I can enjoy the scenery and go deep inside myself to think and pray. The only exception is when it is icy and slippery. On such days, I will go to the fitness center and do some laps around the track. But there are times even in the ice and snow that I will put traction covers over the soles of my running shoes, making them like studded snow tires.

Anyway, getting back to my Christmas Eve run, it was cold and snowy. I took a pause to appreciate the scene. I enjoyed running as the snowflakes fell against my face. I was twenty-six years old at the time and this thought came to me during my run: "I am going to have to do this for the rest of my life." I don't know exactly why that thought came into my mind at that time, except that it seemed related to the fact that my initial motivation for running was to stay physically fit and not die of a heart attack in my mid-fifties. It wasn't a burdensome thought in the sense that it weighed heavily on me; rather, it was more of a simple matter-of-fact reality that I just came to accept as part of my life. You might say it was at that moment of realization that running became a characteristic of who I am. I am a runner.

My third insight involves a personal running tradition I also began early in my priesthood. It too demands a bit of explanation.

St. Michael's was a tri-lingual parish community: English, Polish, and Spanish. The parish was originally founded by immigrants coming from Poland to work in the steel mills, but over the years more and more immigrants came from Mexico, also to work in the steel mills. I had learned some Polish in grade school from the religious sisters of the Congregation of the Resurrection who taught me, but we didn't speak Polish in our fourth-generation home.

Having grown up in a similar tri-lingual parish, St. Casimir Parish, also on the south side of Chicago, I anticipated that someday I would serve as a priest in such a parish. So I took two beginning Spanish courses at Loyola University when I was in the college seminary. Then, after my second year at the major seminary in Mundelein, I went for a seven-week intensive Spanish-language immersion program at Middlebury College in Vermont. I also spent another full summer after my ordination studying Spanish for six weeks in Cuernavaca, Mexico, before arriving to take up my duties at St. Michael's. It was a good thing I had prepared in these ways. By the time I came to St. Michael's, there were more Spanish-speaking parishioners than Poles. In fact, our largest-attended Mass on Sundays was the afternoon Spanish Mass, with more than 1,000 people filling the church. These intensive study experiences served me well, enabling me to celebrate many Masses, weddings, and Baptisms in Spanish and to hear parishioners' confessions in Spanish as well.

A few years later I had to return to Middlebury College to learn another language, Italian. In 1985, I was appointed vice-chancellor of the Archdiocese of Chicago, a position which involved my civil law training. The archbishop of Chicago, Cardinal Joseph Bernardin, noticed that I was also doing quite a bit of canon (church) law in my position so he asked me to go to Rome to study the subject in more depth, which I did at the Pontifical Gregorian University. Before going to Rome, however, I would have to learn Italian. So back to Middlebury College I went.

All of this is setting context for another major decision I made that would greatly impact my life as a runner. The seven-week language program at Middlebury went from the end of June until the middle of August. That meant I would be spending my thirty-fifth birthday on August 5 away from my family and friends at home. What could I do to celebrate on my own? On a whim, I decided I would see how fast I could run a mile at the age of thirty-five! I lined up at the start line on the Middlebury track, turned my baseball cap around backward for greater aerodynamics, and took off as fast as I could run. My time for one mile was six minutes, thirty seconds. Not exactly a world record, but it became an annual benchmark for me. For the next twenty-two years, until I reached the age of fifty-seven, I would go to the track to run my "birthday mile." My goal was to always finish in six minutes, thirty seconds or less, which I achieved every year from August 5, 1987, to August 5, 2009. In fact, my personal record for my birthday mile was five minutes, forty-nine seconds, which I set on July 28, 1999, a week before my forty-seventh birthday.

We runners are creatures of habit. We repeat over and over training and rituals that make us better runners!

Running with the Cows

My time at Middlebury College had another significant impact on my life as a runner—more specifically, as a distance runner. Middlebury College brings in teachers from around the world during the summer for their various language programs. Teachers live in the dormitories along with the students in their respective language groups, facilitating use of the language being studied outside of class time. In fact, the key to the program's success, in my opinion, is Middlebury's "language pledge," by which students promise to speak only the language they're studying for the duration of the seven-week summer intensive program.

According to the language pledge, students were still expected to use the language they were studying, whether in the gym, library, cafeteria, or anywhere else on campus. Violators would be warned after one infraction and would be sent home after repeated infractions. Most of the students took the pledge very seriously. Some were college students majoring in the language they were studying. Many of us were there for professional reasons; for example there were members of the State Department present who would need to learn a language for their jobs in the diplomatic mission to which they were being posted.

I found the language pledge to be very effective. It was also mentally taxing. I had to remember to say "Pass the salt" and everything else in either Spanish during my first stay at Middlebury or Italian in my second summer there. In contrast, when I spent the summer after my ordination to the priesthood studying Spanish in Cuernavaca, Mexico, I was there with several other Americans. Outside of class, we would just slip into speaking English with each other. As a result, to this day I still say that I learned more Spanish during my summer in Vermont than during my summer in Mexico!

How did the language pledge have significant impact on my life as a runner? Simple: running was a great mental break from being forced to converse in a language that was not natural to me. I found this out on my weekend runs in Middlebury. I took refuge in the solitude of long-distance running. As I described in chapter one, I had been running since I was a senior in high school and had gradually been increasing my mileage over the years. So on Sunday afternoons, I would go out by myself and run. That way, I would not have to talk to anyone and risk breaking the language pledge!

Middlebury is a small town, so after a couple of miles, it was just me running along the country roads in the farmlands of New England, gazing along the way at the black and white Holstein cows that Vermont is known for. Just think of the cows on the logo of a carton of Ben & Jerry's ice cream container and you'll have the picture. Spain is known for the running of the bulls. In Vermont, I was running with the cows!

What I discovered on these long runs while giving my brain a break from the language pledge was that I could pretty much run as far as I wanted once I settled into a comfortable pace. So I would go out away from town for at least half an hour and then turn around and head back to campus. It was then that I first got the idea that just maybe I could actually complete the 26.2 miles of a marathon. Eight years later, I would be running in my first Chicago Marathon.

Prayer and the Silence of Running

So what does a long-distance runner do when running for miles and miles and hours and hours? First, I'll tell you what I don't do: I don't wear headphones and listen to music or audiobooks. I tried that years ago back when the first portable cassette players came out. I realize that audio devices and headphones are much more streamlined and compact now than they were back then, but it wasn't really the bulk of carrying an audio device that bothered me so much as the noise. I prefer quiet while I am running. Even when I was doing my weekly marathon training long runs with the pace groups of the Chicago Area Runners Association and speed workouts at Lake Shore Park, most of my daily runs were alone. Perhaps it is the increased flow of oxygen and blood to the brain during intense aerobic exercise, but I found that running was a time for mental problem-solving, literary inspiration, spiritual reflection, and profound prayer.

I discovered during my runs, for example, that solutions to seemingly intractable problems came into clear focus as I thought them through while running. On other occasions, I would not only come up with ideas for homilies and speeches, but I would rehearse them in my mind and commit to memory a general plan of what I wanted to say. I also would think through the outline of an article or chapters of a book that I was writing, such as this one. Most important, and where I spend most of my thought while running in solitude, is deep in prayer. In order to make all these things happen, one needs silence and freedom from distractions.

For some people, silence is a frightening prospect. They cannot fathom the thought of not having some auditory input. In answer to such fears, Cardinal Robert Sarah of Guinea, West Africa, wrote a very helpful book, *The Power of Silence against the Dictatorship of Noise*. In it, he wrote, "A Christian cannot fear silence because he is never alone. . . . In the silence, God gives me eyes so as to contemplate him better. . . . Silence is not frightening, on the contrary, it is the assurance of meeting God" (p. 214). St. Teresa of Calcutta also famously told of the need for silence, saying, "We need to find God, and he cannot be found in noises and restlessness. God is the friend of silence."

You might think that it is only when you are alone that you can experience this kind of silence, but I remember a powerful time of being with a huge crowd of people in absolute silence. It was at World Youth Day in Madrid in 2011, and I was there with some of the young people from our diocese. A powerful storm broke out one evening just as Pope Benedict XVI was about to address those in attendance. Rather than proceed right away, the pope waited until the storm subsided. Then he did something else: he tore up his prepared speech and instead knelt before the Blessed Sacrament in silence. Cardinal Sarah was present at this event too and remembers it this way: "Benedict XVI preached by his silence. There were more than a million young people behind him, drenched to the skin, standing in the mud; nevertheless, over the immense crowd reigned an impressive sacred silence that was literally 'filled with the adored presence.' It is an unforgettable memory, an image of the Church united in great silence around her Lord" (p. 115). Indeed, I will never forget this powerful moment of being united with so many people in silent adoration of our Lord.

Running and Praying the Rosary

Most of my time while running alone is spent in prayer. Not all types of prayer are possible while running. For example, formal liturgical prayer just isn't practical. It is possible, of course, to listen to an audio recording of the scriptures or some spiritual book, but as I said previously, I prefer to run in silence. The types of prayers that I have found most conducive to praying while running are repeated memorized formal or vocal prayers and more spontaneous mental prayers, using the thoughts that come into my mind. Such prayers are formal in the sense of following a predetermined form or text, as opposed to more extemporaneous prayers where one uses his or her own words. They are vocal in that they can be said out loud, rather than in our own thoughts, as we do with mental prayer.

The easiest formalized vocal prayers to remember and pray while running are the prayers of the Rosary, which consists of repeating very familiar prayers, mainly the Lord's Prayer and the Hail Mary. According to Catholic tradition, the history of the Rosary goes back to St. Dominic, who founded the Order of Preachers, more commonly known as the Dominicans, in the thirteenth century. At a time when many people could not read, the repetition of memorized prayers was seen as a substitute for reading the Bible or reciting the Psalms. Saying the Hail Mary 150 times was analogous to reciting the 150 Psalms of the Old Testament. Even though most people today can read the Bible, there is still great merit in repeating prayers for one's spiritual betterment, just as repeated physical exercise makes one's muscles stronger.

A person can keep track of how many prayers he or she is praying by using rosary beads, typically consisting of a number of beads strung together with a cord of thread or metal. A standard set of rosary beads today has a cross with a short string of five beads, then a long string of five sets of ten beads, which is called a decade, separated by a single bead between each decade.

For those who might worry that the repetition of prayers would be monotonous, it may be helpful to understand the repeated saying of the Our Father and Hail Mary prayers as a sort of *mantra*. A mantra is a word or sound repeated to aid concentration in meditation, commonly used in many Eastern religions, such as Hinduism and Buddhism. As we repeat the prayers of the Rosary, we should try to put distracting thoughts out of our minds and concentrate on the words of the prayers and the theme of the mystery of our faith designated for that particular decade of the Rosary.

Once, I gave a set of rosary beads as Christmas gifts to each member of the ice hockey team at the Catholic high school in Springfield, where I assist as a coach. A few weeks later, one of the players who is not Catholic came up to me after a game and said he wanted to talk. We had lost the game, so I thought he might want to vent some about what went wrong with the final outcome. Instead, I was pleasantly surprised when he thanked me for the gift of the rosary beads. He also said he didn't know how to use the beads, so he was wondering if I would show him how to say the Rosary properly. I was happy to do so. I won't presume that all readers of this book will know how to pray the Rosary either, so I will give a brief overview.

Before beginning, you should have in mind an intention for which to pray, such as for someone's health, or for someone out of work to find a job, or for peace and an end to war, or for the repose of the soul of someone who has died. You can also pray for yourself, in atonement for sins you have committed or in thanksgiving for the gifts God has provided to you.

Then, holding the cross, you start with the Sign of the Cross, saying, "In the name of the Father, and of the Son, and of the Holy Spirit," and then recite the Apostles' Creed, as follows:

> I believe in God, the Father Almighty, Creator of Heaven and earth;
> and in Jesus Christ, His only Son Our Lord,
> Who was conceived by the Holy Spirit, born of the Virgin Mary, suffered under Pontius Pilate, was crucified, died, and was buried.
> He descended into Hell; the third day He rose again from the dead;
> He ascended into Heaven, and sits at the right hand of God, the Father almighty; from thence He shall come to judge the living and the dead.
> I believe in the Holy Spirit, the holy Catholic Church, the communion of saints, the forgiveness of sins, the resurrection of the body and life everlasting. Amen.

On the first single bead, you say the Lord's Prayer, that is, the Our Father, praying for the intentions of the Holy Father, in these words which Jesus taught us, which is why it is called the "Lord's Prayer":

> Our Father, who art in heaven, hallowed be thy name. Thy kingdom come, thy will be done, on earth, as it is in heaven. Give us this day our daily bread and forgive us our trespasses as we forgive those who trespass against us; and lead us not into temptation, but deliver us from evil. Amen.

Then, on the next three beads, you say one Hail Mary on each bead, praying for an increase in the virtues of faith, hope, and love. The words of the Hail Mary are as follows:

Hail Mary, Full of Grace, The Lord is with thee. Blessed art thou among women, and blessed is the fruit of thy womb, Jesus. Holy Mary, Mother of God, pray for us sinners now, and at the hour of our death. Amen.

On the next bead, you first say the "Glory be," as follows:

Glory be to the Father, and to the Son, and to the Holy Spirit. As it was in the beginning, is now, and ever shall be, world without end. Amen.

After the "Glory be," you call to mind the "mystery" on which you are to meditate while praying the next decade of the Rosary. I'll say more about the mysteries of the Rosary after explaining what to pray on the rest of the beads.

The decade then begins with the Our Father, followed by ten Hail Mary's, saying one on each bead. At the end of the decade of ten Hail Mary's, you say the "Glory be" again. It has also become customary for many people to say the Fatima Prayer (for the occasion when Mary appeared to three children at Fatima, Portugal in the early twentieth century) as follows:

O my Jesus, forgive us our sins, save us from the fire of hell, lead all souls to heaven, especially those who are in most need of Thy mercy.

That same format is then repeated for the next four decades. After finishing the five decades of the Rosary, you pray the "Hail Holy Queen" prayer in these words:

Hail, holy Queen, mother of mercy, our life, our sweetness, and our hope. To thee do we cry, poor banished children of Eve. To thee do we send up our sighs, mourning and weeping in this valley

of tears. Turn then, most gracious advocate, thine eyes of mercy toward us, and after this our exile show us the blessed fruit of thy womb, Jesus. O clement, O loving, O sweet Virgin Mary. Amen.
Pray for us, O Holy Mother of God.
That we may be made worthy of the promises of Christ.

The following prayer is optional and is said by some either at the start of the Rosary or at the end:

Let us pray. O God, whose Only-Begotten Son, by his life, death and resurrection, has purchased for us the rewards of eternal life, grant, we beseech you, that meditating upon these mysteries of the most holy rosary of the Blessed Virgin Mary, we may imitate what they contain and obtain what they promise, through the same Christ our Lord. Amen.

The Rosary is then concluded by making and reciting the Sign of the Cross.

In the Name of the Father, and of the Son and of the Holy Spirit.

Getting back to the mysteries of the Rosary, the idea is that while we are repeating the Hail Mary prayers of each decade we are reflecting on the truths of our faith, particularly the events of the life of Jesus Christ by which we are saved from our sins. Originally there were three sets of mysteries: the Joyful Mysteries, the Sorrowful Mysteries, and the Glorious Mysteries, with five mysteries in each set. One set of mysteries would be prayed on designated days of the week. On October 16, 2002, Pope St. John Paul II added a new set of five mysteries to the Rosary, known as the

"Luminous Mysteries" or the "Mysteries of Light," focusing on Jesus' public ministry. He also suggested that we meditate on the various mysteries on the different days of the week, designated as follows:

Joyful Mysteries: Monday and Saturday
Luminous Mysteries: Thursday
Sorrowful Mysteries: Tuesday and Friday
Glorious Mysteries: Wednesday and Sunday

Except for the last two decades of the Glorious Mysteries, which honor the Blessed Virgin Mary, the individual mysteries for each decade of the Rosary are based on the life and ministry of Jesus, as follows, with their basis in the Bible indicated in parentheses:

Joyful Mysteries (Monday and Saturday)

1. The Annunciation of Gabriel to Mary (Lk 1:26–38)
2. The Visitation of Mary to Elizabeth (Lk 1:39–56)
3. The Birth of Our Lord (Lk 2:1–21)
4. The Presentation of Our Lord (Lk 2:22–38)
5. The Finding of Jesus in the Temple (Lk 2:41–52)

Sorrowful Mysteries (Tuesday and Friday)

1. The Agony of Our Lord in the Garden (Mt 26:36–56)
2. Jesus Is Scourged at the Pillar (Mt 27:26)
3. Jesus Is Crowned with Thorns (Mt 27:27–31)
4. Jesus Carries the Cross to Calvary (Mt 27:32)
5. The Crucifixion of Our Lord (Mt 27:33–56)

Luminous Mysteries (Thursday)

1. The Baptism of Our Lord in the River Jordan (Mt 3:13–16)
2. The Wedding at Cana, when Christ manifested Himself (Jn 2:1–11)
3. The Proclamation of the Kingdom of God and the call to conversion (Mk 1:14–15)
4. The Transfiguration of Our Lord (Mt 17:1–8)
5. The Last Supper, when Our Lord Gave Us the Holy Eucharist (Mt 26)

Glorious Mysteries (Wednesday and Sunday)

1. The Resurrection of Our Lord (Jn 20:1–29)
2. The Ascension of Our Lord (Lk 24:36–53)
3. The Descent of the Holy Spirit at Pentecost (Acts 2:1–41)
4. The Assumption of Mary into Heaven
5. The Crowning of Mary as Queen of Heaven and Earth

Now, if all of that seems confusing to you and hard to remember, I will give you the same advice I gave to the high school hockey player who asked me to teach him how to pray the Rosary. I told him the best way to learn how to pray the Rosary is actually to pray the Rosary, and so I scheduled a team recitation of the Rosary when all the players came to the chapel at our Catholic Pastoral Center. We prayed the Rosary together. There is a rhythm to the Rosary, and it becomes more familiar the more one prays it. So, if you are new to this, I would suggest you do the same as the hockey player did and not be afraid to ask a Catholic that you know is familiar with the Rosary to teach you how to pray it. I am sure any faithful

Catholic would be flattered by your request and would be more than happy to help you.

Admittedly, until you know the prayers by heart, praying the Rosary while running will be difficult. If that is the case, it might also be wise to listen to an audio recording of the Rosary until you have all the prayers down by heart.

You might have another concern about praying the Rosary while running: how does a runner handle that string of beads while on a run? Good question! The best answer in my opinion is to use a "finger rosary" of ten beads rather than a full rosary of beads. Some finger rosaries are made of metal and some are made of wood, tied together on a string. Personally, I prefer wooden beads on a string. I have some wooden finger rosaries made of olive wood that I bought in Jerusalem and some that I got in Rome and in Assisi, Italy. They are also available online or in person from religious supply stores.

Finger rosaries are easy to use. You simply wrap the finger rosary on your index finger and touch the beads with your thumb.

One of the obvious challenges of using a finger rosary is keeping track of the five decades of the mysteries since you will be carrying only ten beads instead of the usual set of five decades. The best way to remember which decade you are praying is to concentrate on meditating on the particular mystery of the Rosary for that decade. An additional help that I use is to say each decade in one of the five languages that I know: Polish, Italian, Spanish, Latin, and English. I always say them in that order, so I know, for example, if I am saying the Hail Mary's in Spanish, then I am on the third mystery of the Rosary.

You can say a lot of Hail Mary's when you are out there for several hours while doing a long training run or while actually running a marathon. I have even done all four sets of mysteries on a long run or a marathon for a total of two hundred Hail Mary's! Not only can you pray these yourself if you are running alone, but you can say them with others if you are part of a running group of fellow Catholics.

Finally, I mentioned in the previous chapter that I solicited donations for various charitable causes for people to help support my running efforts. When I send out the solicitation letters, I also invite people to send me their prayer intentions. The night before the marathon and right before going to the start line, I will review the prayer requests and keep them in mind while I am running. These requests can also help inspire my running. A prayer request for someone suffering from cancer, for example, is a helpful reminder that the pain of running a few miles pales in comparison to the pain that person is experiencing. It is also an opportunity to join the pain of my running to the suffering of that person, lifting up our suffering to be joined to the passion of Christ, who died on the cross for our sins.

In the next chapter, I will describe some other forms of prayer that help to renew our spirits.

Quotation

"If you say the rosary faithfully unto death, I do assure you that, in spite of the gravity of your sins, "you will receive a never-fading crown of glory."
—St. Louis de Montfort

Promise

I promise to work out repeatedly in order to improve as a runner and to pray repeatedly in order to grow closer to God.

Prayer (the Memorare)

Remember, O most gracious Virgin Mary, that never was it known that anyone who fled to thy protection, implored thy help, or sought thine intercession was left unaided. Inspired by this confidence, I fly unto thee, O Virgin of virgins, my mother; to thee do I come, before thee I stand, sinful and sorrowful. O Mother of the Word Incarnate, despise not my petitions, but in thy mercy hear and answer me. Amen.

5.

Renew

The whole point of running for a higher purpose is to bring about a renewal of physical and spiritual wellness.

So far, we have the first four steps toward spiritual and physical wellness: review, reform, resolve, and repeat. Each of these steps involves making an honest assessment of our situation and our need to improve. Once we have determined where we need to improve, we must identify how to do so. Knowing what to do will not bring about any change unless we resolve to put those steps into effect. Then continued effort is needed lest we quit before seeing any real improvement. We do this, for example, in our physical training by running repeat segments at the track and many miles on our long runs, and in our spiritual exercises by repeating our daily prayers and our weekly Sunday worship. Now we must go deeper and ask: what is the purpose of prayer?

In chapter 4, I described how I pray the Rosary for various intentions while I am running. In this chapter, I will describe some other forms of prayer that I do while running to help to renew my own spirits. Before doing so, however, I should explain why prayer is so important to me while I am running. It is not simply a distraction to keep my mind on other things or away from thinking about the discomfort and pains I may be suffering. The purpose of all prayer is to keep Jesus as the primary focus and center of our lives.

Jesus Is the Focus of Prayer

Quite simply, Jesus is the center of my life. At least, I try to do my part to keep him there. As a sinful and selfish human being, I have a tendency to make myself more important than him. Only God's grace can help me to overcome that self-centered tendency, so in that sense Jesus is my Lord and Savior because he saves me from selfishness.

How did I come to first know Jesus? My relationship with Jesus came about primarily through the beautiful example of my parents, the priests they knew, and the religious sisters who taught me in grade school. It grew over the years, thanks to the mentoring of some wonderful priests and bishops that I met when I was a seminarian and then after I was ordained a priest.

Two archbishops of Chicago were especially instrumental is teaching me how to have a close relationship with Jesus. Cardinal Joseph Bernardin was archbishop of Chicago from 1982 to 1996. I served as his chancellor from 1992 until his death in 1996, and I heard him speak often about how he would wake up early every morning and spend the first hour of his day in prayer. In his book, *The Gift of Peace*, which he completed shortly before he died, Cardinal Bernardin explained this practice:

> I decided to give God the first hour of my day, no matter what, to be with him in prayer and meditation where I would try to open the door even wider to his entrance. This put my life into a new and uplifting perspective.

When Cardinal Bernardin died, I served his successor, Cardinal Francis George, also as chancellor of the Archdiocese as well as a pastor of a parish and auxiliary bishop. He was also later my metropolitan archbishop in my capacity as bishop of the Diocese of Springfield in Illinois. Springfield is part of the larger ecclesiastical Province of Chicago. I also learned a great deal from him, both in frequent conversations and by reading his scholarly writings.

Cardinal George, in the days just before he died, also finished a book titled *A Godly Humanism: Clarifying the Hope that Lies Within*. From Cardinal George I took two important lessons to heart: Jesus' promise that "the truth shall make you free" and that Jesus founded the Church as the repository of truth and hence, as the place where we find true freedom. Cardinal George explained it this way:

> Jesus promised that "The truth shall make you free," but where objective truth is regarded as the enemy of human liberty, many will abandon truth even though they ultimately forfeit liberty as a consequence, for we can't be free if cut off from the truth of things. To live in falsehood is to live beneath human dignity, in the space where emancipation is meaningless. That confronts us with the most culturally outrageous statement that can be made in our time; but it is true: The Church is where you go when you want to be free.

In short, peace and truth make us free, and freedom leads to love, for when we are free, we find God, who is Love, and this Love gives us the grace we need to love each other. Keeping Jesus at the center of my life is the best way to fulfill the two-fold commandment to love God and neighbor.

I was blessed to have exemplary mentors like Cardinal Bernardin and Cardinal George who modeled for me how to have a loving relationship with the Lord. Not everyone has been so fortunate. I have heard many life-long Catholics, both laity and priests, say that they do not know what it means to have a relationship with Jesus Christ. They have been faithful, practicing Catholics for many years, but they tell me that the idea of a "relationship" with Jesus is hard to fathom when they cannot see Jesus the way they see a person who is physically present to them. In response to such uncertainties, I would say that you can have a relationship with Jesus to the extent that you can relate to him by conversation (prayer), intimacy (Holy Communion), spending time in his presence (eucharistic adoration and contemplation) and, most importantly, receiving his love and loving him in return. I find all of these ways essential to my relationship with the Lord.

Prayer is indispensable for maintaining and deepening this relationship. I try to begin each day with prayer *and* physical exercise. Some of those prayers are prayed in my private chapel at the cathedral rectory where I reside, many are offered in churches as part of formal liturgical ceremonies, and others are offered in my own words in various contexts of informal conversation with God, such as when I am driving in my car or when I go running.

Start the Day with Prayer While Running!

I usually wake up about five every morning, sometimes earlier, sometimes later, to get my running in. It all depends on how far I plan to run that day. Don't get me wrong: I am not one of those naturally chipper morning people who bounce out of bed with eager enthusiasm for the day. My father was a morning person. He would tell us how he would wake up the bugler to play "Reveille" on the trumpet to rouse the rest of the troops when he served as a sergeant in the army during World War II.

I did not get those early morning genes. In this regard, I am more like my mother. Someone remarked to me once that my mother must have been super busy every morning getting nine children ready for school. I replied, "No, my mother was usually still in bed when I went to school!" It was my father who woke us up, made sure we got dressed, prepared our breakfast, and sent us off to school on time. This does not mean that my mother was shirking any duty. Quite the contrary: Mom was a stay-at-home mother, cooking delicious meals every day and taking care of the household. She was also wide-awake at the end of the day to help us with our homework, while Dad was fading off after a long day of working at his pharmacy and heading off to bed early. So Mom and Dad complemented each other well in this regard. Dad was the morning person and Mom was the night person, so our family was well cared-for at both ends of the day.

I am also more like my mother in terms of natural inclination. By that I mean that my natural inclination is to stay up late and sleep late. I thrived on that schedule when I was in college. But once I was ordained a priest and was also attending law school, my daily routine had to change. I still did my best studying and writing at night, but I also had to get up early to celebrate Mass and get to class. So I became a morning person by design. It was not easy.

Someone asked Pope St. John Paul II how he woke up in the morning. He answered, "With difficulty." That would be an apt description for me as well. I force myself to wake up. St. Josemaría Escrivá, a Spanish priest of the twentieth century and founder of Opus Dei (Work of God), an organization for priests and laity, called this the "heroic minute," forcing yourself to get out of bed right at the designated time. He described it this way:

> Conquer yourself each day from the very first
> moment, getting up on the dot, at a fixed time,
> without yielding a single minute to laziness. If,
> with God's help, you conquer yourself, you will be
> well ahead for the rest of the day. . . . The heroic
> minute. It is the time fixed for getting up. Without
> hesitation: a supernatural reflection and . . . up!
> The heroic minute: here you have a mortification
> that strengthens your will and does no harm to
> your body.

Of course, jumping out of bed at the "heroic minute"
means getting to bed and asleep at a decent hour the night
before. This takes discipline too. There are always more
e-mails to send, notes to write, articles and books to read, various forms of social media to peruse, and, of course, sporting
events on television. The challenge is to set a regular time to
go to bed and then to keep it even when you don't feel ready
for sleep. After a while, your body clock of circadian rhythms
starts to adjust, and it is easier to fall right to sleep and get
up when the alarm goes off in the morning. Actually, I never
have much trouble falling asleep. Keeping a full schedule and
regular exercise help to ensure that I fall sound asleep within
a few minutes of my head hitting the pillow.

When I was younger and had a more predictable schedule,
I preferred to run in the late afternoon before supper. That
changed after my ordination when more unexpected demands
were being put upon my time. When somebody shows up
at the parish office just minutes before your scheduled run
and says, "Father, I really need to talk to you," it's not a good
idea to say, "Sorry, but I'm going running now. Can you come
back later?" So I found that the best time that I could plan on
going running without interruption was the first thing in the
morning.

I soon discovered a great benefit of running in the morning. Running helps me to wake up! I gave up caffeine in 1989 (I'll say more about that in the next chapter), and have been caffeine-free ever since, so I can't rely on a morning cup of coffee to get me going. What I found, though, is even if I'm dragging myself out the door and am feeling sluggish at the start of my run, within about a half mile, the blood and oxygen are flowing through my body and I feel wide-awake.

As I mentioned, I combine running with prayer. I see nothing wrong with that. I remember years ago when I was in the seminary, when smoking cigarettes was very much still in vogue, someone asked a Jesuit priest if it was all right to smoke a cigarette while praying. He answered, in classic Jesuit fashion, "No, but it's all right to pray while you're smoking." Likewise, it would not be all right for me to be running while leading prayers in church, but there's nothing wrong with praying while running!

As I start my run, I begin my prayer with these words:

> I come to you this morning, Lord, with praise and thanksgiving for all that I am and all that I have. I offer to you all that I will do this day. Please be with me and guide me. Fill me with the spirit of your wisdom and love.

Then I offer what I would describe as my personal litany of prayers, praying for various groups of people, many of them by name:

- I pray for the Church throughout the world, the pope, bishops, priests, deacons, consecrated religious, seminarians, and prospective seminarians.
- I pray for all the people of our diocese, my family, and my friends.

- I pray for those suffering from poverty, sickness, grief, war terrorism, genocide, and natural disasters.

- I pray for peace and justice as well as the protection of all life from conception to natural death.

- I pray for vocations to the priesthood, religious life, and the Sacrament of Matrimony.

- I pray for bishops, priests, and deacons who are guilty or accused of sexual misconduct or financial misconduct.

- I pray for healing for the victims of sexual abuse.

- I pray for those in the legal system who decipher the truth and administer justice.

- I pray for all those who have asked for my prayers and for those to whom I have promised my prayers.

- I pray for the repose of the souls of those who have died, that they might rest in peace.

- I pray for myself to be a better person, a better Christian, and a better priest and bishop.

I conclude my litany with these words:

> Lord, please be the center of my life: my mind and heart, my thoughts and feelings, my words and actions; all that I think, all that I say and all that I do. For I love you, Lord, and I pray to you with great longing and hope that you will welcome me with open arms into your loving embrace in that Kingdom where you live and reign forever and ever. Amen.

As I described in the previous chapter, I usually carry a small finger rosary of ten beads to pray the Rosary while I am running. After I finish my personal litany of prayers for various people, I pray at least a decade of the Rosary or more, depending on how long I will be running. Then, depending again how much time I have left for that run, I use a traditional form of prayer known as mental prayer.

Mental Prayer

Defined simply, mental prayer is a loving conversation with the Lord. It differs from formal, memorized prayers, like the Our Father and Hail Mary that we pray in the Rosary, in that we use our own words. It is mental prayer as contrasted to vocal prayer in that the words do not need to be vocalized or spoken out loud, but may be expressed to God in the silent thoughts of our mind. Fr. John Hardon, SJ, once described mental prayer as a "form of prayer in which the sentiments expressed are one's own and not those of another person. Mental prayer is accomplished by internal acts of the mind and affections and is either simple meditation or contemplation." As all conversations are a two-way interaction, God does speak to us in mental prayer as well, usually in the quiet thoughts of our mind. I will give you an example a little later of how that has worked for me.

First, though, let me give you some suggestions of an outline of what to say to God in your mental prayer. St. Josemaría Escrivá recommended beginning mental prayer by situating ourselves in relation with the Holy Family of Jesus, Mary, and Joseph. He recommended beginning mental prayer with this invocation:

> My Lord and my God, I firmly believe that you are here; that you see me, that you hear me. I adore you with profound reverence; I beg your pardon for my sins, and the grace to make this time of prayer fruitful. My Immaculate Mother, St, Joseph my father and lord, my guardian angel, intercede for me.

Having started our mental prayer in the context of the Holy Family, we should see ourselves as beloved sons and daughters of God, with whom we now enter into this loving conversation.

There are different kinds of mental prayer. *Meditation* involves reflecting or thinking about some passage of the Bible or some article of faith, such as the real presence of Jesus in the Eucharist or the gifts of the Holy Spirit. This can be done while running by simply calling to mind some scripture passage you have memorized or some particular teaching of the Church with which you are familiar. You can also prepare for meditation while running by reading a scripture passage or a paragraph from the *Catechism of the Catholic Church* before you go out the door to start your run.

Contemplation is another form of mental prayer. It was defined by St. Teresa of Avila as "nothing else than a close sharing between friends; it means taking time frequently to be alone with him who we know loves us." Contemplation can also be done while running, by focusing more on the affections of God's love for us and our love for him rather than thinking about the deeper mysteries of our faith.

ACTS: An Acronym for Mental Prayer

While running is conducive to meditation and contemplation, I usually spend more of my time just talking with God in my thoughts as the miles go by. The common agenda of topics for this conversation can easily be summarized and remembered with the acronym, ACTS, which stands for **A**doration, **C**ontrition, **T**hanksgiving, and **S**upplication. Each of these topics can be prayed as long or short as you want. You don't have to do all of them on one run. Here is more explanation of each topic:

- *Adoration* is giving praise and glory to God. We offer our adoration to God in the three divine persons of the Holy Trinity: Father, Son, and Holy Spirit, by which God has created us, redeemed us from our sins, and sustains us with his grace on our journey to eternal life.

- *Contrition* is expressing sorrow and repentance for our sins, asking for God's mercy and forgiveness. We could do this in a general sense or in the form of a more detailed examination of conscience, such as thinking of the events of the previous day or week and calling to mind specific instances of knowingly and willfully breaking one of the Ten Commandments or precepts of the Church, or other ways that we may have offended God or harmed another person. We should make an act of contrition asking God's forgiveness for our sins, and if any of these are mortal (serious) sins, we should resolve to go to confession and receive absolution from a priest in the Sacrament of Penance and Reconciliation. An act of contrition may be expressed in one's own words, just telling God you are sorry for your sins and asking for his forgiveness, or it can be said using a memorized formula. The one I learned as a child and still say as an adult is the following:

    > O my God, I am heartily sorry for having offended Thee, and I detest all my sins because of Thy just punishments, but most of all because they offend Thee, my God, Who art all-good and deserving of all my love. I firmly resolve, with the help of Thy grace, to sin no more and to avoid the near occasions of sin. Amen.

- *Thanksgiving* is expressing gratitude and appreciation to God for all of the gifts you have received from him. Once again, as with contrition, I think it is best to be specific and detailed when giving thanks to God. I also recommend offering your prayers of thanksgiving before you start telling God all of your problems and asking for solutions for them. I do this by thinking of the events of the previous day and saying thank you to God for the people I encountered, mentioning them by name, and expressing gratitude for various good things that happened to me. Our human tendency seems for us to be acutely aware of how people may have hurt us, or where things have gone poorly, or not as we had hoped or expected. If I start by giving thanks for the people and good things in my life, my spirits are lifted, I feel spiritually renewed, and then the hurts and problems with which I had been so preoccupied seem diminished and less burdensome.

• *Supplication* means to ask for something earnestly or humbly. Prayers of supplication are also called prayers of petition and intercessory prayers. In fact, this seems to be our default setting for prayer. We are always asking God for something, either for ourselves or others. We pray for success in some challenge or task we have to do, we ask for healing for ourselves and others in time of sickness, and we pray for the repose of the souls of those who have died. As I get older, the list of loved ones who have died keeps getting longer and longer, and my intercessory prayer for them not only helps them if they are still in need of remission of the temporal punishment for sins they committed while on earth, but praying for them also keeps them close in my thoughts and affections for them.

By now you may have noticed that most of my prayers seem to be pretty one-sided, that is, with me doing most of the talking, either offering my personal litany for various people, praying the Rosary, or talking to God in my own words with prayers of adoration, contrition, thanksgiving, and supplication. I also tend to realize the same thing at some point in my praying while running, and so I make a conscious effort to stop talking and start listening.

Listening to God

I start the process of listening to God in prayer by speaking a few more words. I say:

> I open my mind and my thoughts, my heart and my soul, to you, O Lord, to whatever you wish to communicate to me in this time of prayer, through the intercession of your most Blessed Mother and St. Joseph, her most chaste spouse.

I then make this specific request, using the words of the prophet Samuel from the Old Testament: "Speak, Lord, for your servant is listening" (1 Sm 3:10). Then, I try just to listen.

More often than not, in all honesty, what I hear is silence. That is not a bad thing, although in our noisy world, we are not used to silence and may in fact be uncomfortable with it. But silence is necessary if we hope to encounter God. Nevertheless, there are times when God does communicate clearly with us. I will tell you how I have experienced God communicating to me while running.

In the occasion I want to share, I was in the last couple of miles of a twenty-mile marathon training long run. I was running on the Lost Bridge Trail in Springfield, which extends from behind the Illinois Department of Transportation building along a five-mile stretch to the town of Rochester. It is an old railway bed, so it is flat and straight, with lots of trees along both sides of the trail providing shade from the hot summer sun. So a twenty-mile long run means going out and back twice on the five-mile trail.

Realizing that again I had been doing most of the talking in my prayer, I invited the Lord to talk to me: "Speak, Lord, for your servant is listening." Almost immediately, the thought came into my mind, "Hold fast to the cross." Now, I was literally holding my finger rosary on my index finger with my thumb on the cross. Often, when I make the transition from praying the Rosary to mental prayer, I put the finger rosary in my pocket. I was about to do that when I heard the message, "Hold fast to the cross." So I thought, okay, I should just keep the rosary on my finger with my thumb on the cross. Why? Maybe Jesus was reminding me of his words, "Whoever wishes to come after me must deny himself, take up his cross, and follow me" (Mt 16:24).

Then, almost immediately, I heard another thought come into my mind: "Embrace the pain." Now I clearly had the feeling that this was not a matter of me talking to myself because embracing pain was the last thing I wanted to do! At that point I was in the last mile of my twenty-mile long run, my muscles were screaming with fatigue and my body was sore all over, so my prayer in my own words would have been "Lord, take away this pain." So when I heard, "Embrace the pain," I practically yelled, "No, that's not what I want to hear now!" Then I realized that this thought must have come from somewhere outside of me. The scriptures do speak often of the sufferings that we must endure. I thought of the words in the first letter of Peter: "Beloved, do not be surprised that a trial by fire is occurring among you, as if something strange were happening to you. But rejoice to the extent that you share in the sufferings of Christ, so that when his glory is revealed you may also rejoice exultantly" (1 Pt 4:12–13).

For several months after that, I basically heard the same message while running whenever I would invite God to speak to me: "Hold fast to the cross. . . . Embrace the pain." That was all I heard.

Then one day, out of nowhere, came another thought: "Do not complain." Could this be God speaking to me again? My own reaction was, "What? You want me to embrace the pain, and then not even complain about it?" I took the silence to mean God affirming his "yes" to my question.

Several more months went by. Then, added to the previous messages came another thought: "Be cheerful." I tried to put all the messages together. It seemed that God wanted me to hold fast to the cross and embrace its pain without complaint. And the latest message seemed to mean that I should actually be cheerful while doing so! Once again, I took the silent response to be God's affirmation. I have thought and prayed a lot about what the total message could mean. I have come to understand cheerfulness as a type of self-mortification. By that I mean that it is easy to wallow in self-pity and let others know when we're feeling miserable. Unlike happiness and joy, which are interior dispositions that arise naturally, cheerfulness is an attitude that we can and should consciously adopt even when we are not feeling particularly happy or joyful. I used to wonder if I was being hypocritical if I smiled and tried to be friendly even if I felt that I was in a bad mood, but I have come to see that people have enough of their own problems to deal with, so they don't need grumpiness from me. Being cheerful when I don't feel like it is a mortification and a sacrifice in that it involves dying to my own self-pity and trying to bring some cheerfulness into someone else's life who may need it more than I do.

Essential Prayers Apart from Running

The prayers I have been describing so far can be said while running: praying the Rosary and engaging in mental prayer. There are two other essential types of prayer that are not truly feasible while running, but they must be mentioned because no prayer life is complete without them. They are reading the Bible and celebrating the Eucharist.

Let's talk about reading the Bible first. The Church refers both to the Bible and to Christ as the Word of God. In that sense, if you want to know Christ who is the Word of God incarnate in the world, you must know the Bible, which is God's Word speaking to us through the inspiration of the Holy Spirit.

The most direct approach to praying with the Bible, of course, is simply to sit down and read some passages on a frequent, if not daily basis. I do not do this as often as I would like, since so much of my contact with the Bible involves preparing homilies based on assigned passages of scripture according to the cycle of readings found in the Lectionary. In the course of doing so, however, I often look at the passages immediately preceding and following the section designated for the liturgy in order to get a fuller sense of the context of the passage. Sometimes I will take a particular book of the Bible and read a brief passage every morning until I go through the whole book from start to finish, for example, the book of the prophet Isaiah during Advent or the Acts of the Apostles during the Easter season. I find that reading in this way gives me a better feel for the overall message of that book or epistle that is not always immediately apparent when I read just one section apart from the rest.

When I was ordained a deacon, in addition to promising celibacy and obedience to my bishop and his successors, I promised to pray the Liturgy of the Hours daily. The Liturgy of the Hours is also called the "breviary" or "Divine Office" (from the Latin word *officium*, which means "duty"). The title Liturgy of the Hours more aptly signifies that these are prayers to be offered throughout the various hours of the day at morning, midday, evening, and at night. All of the hours of the liturgy are basically from the Bible, with emphasis placed on the recitation of the Psalms. Faithfully praying the Liturgy of the Hours on a daily basis certainly helps to keep me in touch with the Word of God.

I shouldn't really say that praying with the Bible is completely unfeasible while running. This is mostly the case for me since I do not like to wear headphones or earbuds while running. But if you are used to listening to music or audible books while running, then I would suggest that you add the Bible to your audio collection. There are good Bible apps that you can use with your listening device. *The Truth and Life Catholic Bible App*, produced by Mike Stark, is a free download, complete with movie-quality sound effects and an original music score. This audio New Testament is endorsed with an Imprimatur from the Vatican and includes a foreword by Pope emeritus Benedict XVI. It is voiced by many renowned actors and is available from Truth and Life, a main producer of audio Bibles.

I do run with the Bible in a way. In preparing my homilies for Sunday Mass and researching their exegetical meaning of the readings, sometimes I will reread the liturgical readings right before I go out running so that I can think about the scripture passages assigned for the coming Sunday and begin to get some ideas for my homily. So while praying with the Bible is mostly not conducive to running, it is possible, even for someone who doesn't run with earbuds like me!

The Importance of the Eucharist

One of the more ironic phrases I have heard from people who have left the Catholic Church and joined an evangelical Protestant denomination is that they felt they "were not being fed" in the Catholic Church. I say this is ironic since they are leaving the Church where they are literally fed and nourished with the Body of Christ in Holy Communion and then join a community that has no opportunity for them to receive the real presence of Christ in Eucharist. In this case, I would say that they are only getting half a loaf. The full loaf of spiritual bread is word and sacrament, which is what the Catholic Church as instituted by Christ provides. The Mass itself has two parts, the Liturgy of the Word and the Liturgy of the Eucharist.

What is the meaning of *sacrament*? The basic definition that I learned as a boy from the *Baltimore Catechism* is that a "sacrament is an outward sign instituted by Christ to give grace." The grace we receive in the sacraments is simply God's loving presence and his strength to assist us in living a life of virtue and holiness. Frequent reception of the Sacraments of Penance and Reconciliation and the Eucharist, especially, helps us to maintain a close relationship with Jesus.

I do not like to recommend something unless I am willing to do it myself. In that regard, I normally go to sacramental confession twice a month. Some may object that they do not commit many mortal sins and so do not need to go to confession that often. While Catholics are required to always confess mortal sins before receiving Holy Communion and to participate in the Sacrament of Penance and Reconciliation at least once a year, I find that frequent confession of venial sins helps my love and devotion for Jesus to grow deeper. Comparing our relationship with Jesus to a relationship with anyone else, we cannot expect to grow in that relationship if we only say we are sorry when there is a complete rupture, which is what mortal sin does to our relationship with God. We must also pay attention to the times when the relationship is merely strained so that the bonds of love and friendship can be strengthened.

After receiving Holy Communion at Mass, it is customary to spend some time in quiet thanksgiving to God. There are no prescribed prayers for this, because the whole idea is to talk to God in our own words in the intimacy of a personal conversation with our loving Lord who has just come into our hearts. My personal post-communion prayer of thanksgiving is usually along these lines:

> Lord, please accept this Mass and Communion that I offer to you as a sign of repentance for my sins, as an expression of love, and as an act of thanksgiving for your many, many gifts. May your Body and Blood transform our body and blood so that we may be a true Corpus Christi and I may be an authentic Alter Christus, and we may be more loving members of your Mystical Body. I come to you, Lord, with a heart full of thanks: I thank you for life, for health, for work, for play, for family and for friends. I thank you for your love and for your presence in this Eucharist. Please be with me not only now, but until I have the grace to receive you again.

Related to our celebration of the holy Mass is Eucharistic Adoration. Praying before the Blessed Sacrament allows us to bask in the presence of Jesus and is another way to strengthen our relationship with him. Through the practice of mental prayer at Eucharistic Adoration, I tell the Lord what is on my mind, thanking him for the blessings of the previous day and asking for his guidance in whatever tasks await me. It is also a time for me to simply be quiet and listen. I try to open my mind and my thoughts, my heart and my soul, to Christ and his Blessed Mother, to be receptive to whatever they wish to communicate to me. As I do when I am running, when I pray before the Blessed Sacrament I say as Samuel did in the Old Testament: "Speak Lord, for your servant is listening" (1 Sm 3:10).

Spiritual communion is also an effective practice to deepen your intimacy with the Lord when you are not able to go to Holy Communion for whatever reason. It could be that you are conscious of grave sin and have not had the opportunity to go to sacramental confession and receive absolution. It may simply be that you have eaten something right before Mass and thus have not observed the required one-hour fast before receiving Holy Communion. Many people became aware of the practice of spiritual communion during the coronavirus pandemic when public Masses were not held for a number of weeks. A spiritual communion is appropriate for times you desire to be with Jesus in a deeper way. You can also make a spiritual communion while you are running! A recommended Act of Spiritual Communion was composed by St. Alphonsus Liguori in the eighteenth century:

> My Jesus, I believe that you are present in the Blessed Sacrament. I love you above all things and I desire you with all my heart. Since I cannot now receive you sacramentally, I ask you to come spiritually into my heart. I embrace you as if you were already in my heart and unite myself to you completely. Please do not let me ever be separated from you.

There is no official prayer for making a spiritual communion, however. People can use their own words to express a longing or desire for Christ to come spiritually into their heart. I do this, for example, when I have just a few minutes to visit our Lord in the tabernacle in my private chapel at the cathedral rectory or the St. Viator Chapel at the Catholic Pastoral Center, saying something like, "Lord, it is good to be with you and I desire for you to remain in my heart." When passing any Catholic church, I bow my head or tip my hat (if I am wearing one, such as my White Sox baseball cap, which

I usually wear while running) as I make the Sign of the Cross and say, "Blessed be God in the Most Holy Sacrament of the altar." My father taught me to do this when I was a little boy and would go with him for a walk. This practice has stayed with me ever since!

Even though one cannot celebrate the Mass while running, I do see a connection between the spiritual renewal that we receive from the Eucharist and the motivation to engage well in our daily activities, which includes running. In fact, the word Mass comes from the Latin word *missa*, which means "to send or dispatch." The word "missal" and "dismissal" also derive from this Latin word, since a person who has attended Mass is then dismissed or sent forth with the words *Ite missa est,* that is, "Go, it [the Eucharist] is sent" with you into the world to bring the presence of the Christ's love received at Mass into your daily activities and encounters with others. This is seen more clearly in the new English translation of the Roman Missal, which includes these words of dismissal at the end of Mass: "Go and announce the Gospel of the Lord" or "Go in peace, glorifying the Lord by your life."

There are many means available to us—such as prayers, reading the Bible, and receiving the Eucharist—that help to bring about a renewal of physical and spiritual wellness in our lives. Combining spiritual exercises with physical training may seem like a lot of work and, in a sense, it is a lot of work that consumes much physical, mental, and emotional energy. For that reason, we must also find ways to rest and relax, which will be the focus of the next chapter.

Quotation

"I urge you therefore . . . to offer your bodies as a living sacrifice, holy and pleasing to God, your spiritual worship. Do not conform yourselves to this age but be transformed by the renewal of your mind, that you may discern what is the will of God, what is good and pleasing and perfect."

—St. Paul in the letter to the Romans (12:1–2)

Promise

I promise to use the means available to me—such as prayer, reading the Bible, and receiving the Eucharist—to help to bring about a renewal of physical and spiritual wellness in my life.

Prayer

O God, out of love for us you have given us the Church and the sacraments to renew our spiritual lives. May these gifts strengthen us in body and soul so that we might discern God's will, what is good and pleasing and perfect. We ask this through Christ our Lord. Amen.

6.

Relax

Physical exercise and spiritual exercises are both hard work, but effort must be balanced with rest to prevent burnout.

You may have noticed that each chapter of this book starts with a word beginning with the letter *R*: review, reform, resolve, repeat, renew, relax, rejoice, and reward. The prefix *re*, which means "back" or "again," appears in hundreds of English vocabulary words, for example: re-gain, re-turn, and re-vert. In a sense, the path to spiritual and physical wellness should take us back to resemble more closely the primordial or original state of our bodies and souls as created by God. That will only happen in perfection when our bodies are resurrected—re-surrected (*surrexit* is Latin for "raised up")—on the last day when Christ comes in all his glory to raise up our bodies in glorified form.

When I celebrate the Sacrament of Confirmation, I often include in my homily an explanation of our Christian belief in the resurrection of the body, which we profess in the renewal of baptismal promises at Confirmation. We believe that our bodies will be raised up one day in a glorified form similar to our Lord's glorified body when he rose from the dead. That means that in the future our bodies will be freed from all sicknesses, diseases, infirmities, and disabilities. At one particular Confirmation, as I shared these words, a young man seated below me in a wheelchair let out a loud cheer. The surprised congregation briefly gasped, then joined in the cheering with him! Yes, the resurrection of our bodies is something to shout about, and it especially gave this young man hope to look forward to the day when he would have a healthy and holy body that would no longer be confined to his wheelchair.

This chapter, titled "Relax," could also have a number of subcategories of words that start with the letter R and the prefix "re"—rest, recover, replenish, refresh, repair, renew, and more. So how do we go about recharging our batteries (another re- word!)? We will take a look at various ways to balance the hard work of spiritual and physical exercise with rest and recovery to prevent burnout.

Resting in God

We don't have to look any further than the first book of the Bible to find a scriptural basis for rest (and relaxation). In the book of Genesis, creation takes place over a span of six days, and God "rested on the seventh day from all the work He had undertaken" (Gn 2:2). Why did God rest? As God, he is almighty and all powerful, so it could not be that he was tired. Perhaps he rested simply to give us an example of what we are to do: we should keep a Sabbath day, a day of rest, once per week. Let's look more closely at the meaning of the Sabbath.

When God gave Moses the Ten Commandments, he commanded that the Sabbath be kept holy and that it was to be observed on the seventh day of the week, following God's example of resting on the seventh day after the six days of creation. By its nature, the Sabbath is to be a day of prayer and worship of God, as well as a day of rest. The word "sabbatical" has its root in the word "Sabbath," since a sabbatical is a respite from one's responsibilities of work for a period of time to get refreshed and renewed. The different branches of Judaism observe the Sabbath rest to varying degrees, some stricter than others. Jewish people continue to keep Saturday as the Sabbath.

Christians, however, from the earliest days of the Church have kept the Lord's Day on Sunday, in commemoration of the fact that Jesus rose from the dead on a Sunday, the third day after his crucifixion. For Catholics, Sunday is a holy day of obligation, meaning that one is obliged to attend Mass under consequences of mortal sin. However, it is more spiritually beneficial and efficacious if a person participates in the holy sacrifice of the Mass not only out of a sense of obligation and avoidance of sin, but more importantly, as a way to worship God, to love and adore him, and to receive the loving presence of Christ into our hearts in the Eucharist.

The duty to rest on Sunday should also be observed in a similar spirit. It is not just a question of avoiding your regular job as part of the obligation of Sunday rest, but to see Sunday as a day that should be different from the rest of the work week. For example, there's nothing wrong with texting or e-mailing on Sundays, but these messages should be in the spirit of friendship and extended mainly to family and friends. Similarly, there's nothing wrong with reading or watching television on Sunday, but those activities should ideally be done with family members nearby.

What about Running on Sundays?

Then there's the question of running on Sunday: is running work or recreation? An argument could be made either way. If you experience running as a painful exertion of effort, maybe it would be better for you to use Sunday as a rest day from running. On the other hand, if running is a social occasion to put in a few miles with friends or if you just like the experience of getting a "runner's high" that comes from the flow of blood and oxygen and the release of endorphins in your brain, then maybe running is more of a recreational activity for you.

In the marathon training program from Hal Higdon that I included in chapter 2, we saw that there are two full rest days built into the novice training program. The schedules for intermediate and advanced runners usually include fewer rest days. Because I have been running for so many years, I find that I need fewer full days off from running and may not even need a day off every week. I often go ten days or so before taking a day off. Recently, I ran every day for over a month. Now, that does not mean I run the same distance or with the same intensity every day. Because running in the morning refreshes me and wakes me up, a rest day for me may be cutting back to doing just a light one or two-mile jog, rather than not running at all.

In my marathon training, Saturday has almost always been the day for my weekly long run. The exceptions have been when I have a Confirmation or other special Mass scheduled on a Saturday morning, so then I will do my long run either on Friday or Sunday evening. Saturday morning is also typically a better time for me as a priest, because Sunday morning is when I am usually scheduled to celebrate Mass.

The schedule of the Chicago Area Runners' Association shows that most runners prefer to do their weekly marathon training long run on Saturday mornings as well. For some, that may be for a purely practical reason. If you do your long run on Saturday morning, you can go out and have a good time on Saturday night! It really dampens one's plans for a night out if you know you have to put in fifteen to twenty miles the next morning. I would think, however, that religious reasons may also be a factor for many runners who want to go to church on Sunday morning. For Catholics, Sunday morning long runs are not automatically excluded due to the fact that many parishes offer Masses on the Saturday vigil and Sunday evenings that fulfill the Sunday Mass obligation.

Now, when it comes to the marathon race itself, most marathons take place on Sunday mornings. For me, that means planning ahead and scheduling my Mass for Saturday evening instead of Sunday morning. Nearly every fall, I run a marathon in a different part of the country as part of my support for the LIFE Runners, a pro-life running organization, founded by Dr. Patrick Castle, a retired Air Force Colonel. Even away from home, I try to keep the same routine. Our typical schedule on a marathon weekend is to attend the sponsor's expo most races hold on Saturday morning. The LIFE Runners organization hosts a booth with information about our activities and to sign up new members. On Saturday afternoon, we go to an abortion facility where we pray the Rosary on behalf of the pregnant mothers and their children. Next, we go to a local Catholic church, where I celebrate Mass. Our night concludes with a pre-race pasta dinner attended by the LIFE Runners and their families and friends. Then it's time to get some sleep! We all gather again on Sunday morning shortly before the start of the race near the starting line for a pre-race prayer and blessing. From there, it's off to the race!

When I was living at Holy Name Cathedral's rectory in Chicago, I once asked race officials of the Chicago Marathon if the race could be moved from Sunday to Saturday morning, not only for the sake of my own Mass schedule, but because the marathon course went right past the cathedral and several other churches along the way, obstructing churchgoers from getting to services. I was told that city officials would not permit that since a marathon on Saturday morning would be too disruptive for businesses and consumers. Oh well, I thought. I guess that's a sign of how secular and consumeristic our culture has become, when it is all right to disrupt churchgoers from trying to get to their worship services on Sunday morning, but heaven help us if we were to disrupt shoppers from getting to the stores to spend money on Saturday!

Fortunately, there are some marathons that I have participated in that are held on Saturday morning, such as the Indianapolis Marathon and the Air Force Marathon at Wright-Patterson Air Force Base in Dayton, Ohio. I wish more marathons would follow their example.

More about the Importance of Sleep

We cannot think about relaxing, resting and recovery without mentioning more about the importance of sleep. The consensus of experts who have studied the science of sleep is that most people need seven to eight hours of sleep per night. There are some exceptions for those who can get by on less sleep and some who need more. The fact that these are exceptions to the rule does not make these exceptional people. Yet our workaholic society tends to glorify people who can get by on just a few hours of sleep as role models for others to emulate. In fact, many people who try to get by on less are simply sleep-deprived.

Although most people need seven to eight hours of sleep per night, the reality is that this is not always possible. If you recall my earlier description of how I was going full-time to law school while working full-time as a parish priest, starting with 6:30 Mass in the morning and staying up to study until midnight, you can rightly assume I was getting by on about six hours of sleep per night, but I was not running marathons in those years, either.

When I became bishop of Springfield in Illinois, I had a similar schedule. I enrolled in the Executive Masters in Business Administration program at the Mendoza College of Business of the University of Notre Dame. Classes were held at the Chicago Commons all day Friday and Saturday every other weekend for a year and a half, from January of 2012 to May of 2013. At the same time, I was keeping to a full schedule of Confirmation Masses and other responsibilities as diocesan bishop. Also, I was training for and running in the St. Louis Marathon in 2012 and the Springfield Marathon in 2013. So it was not uncommon for me to be getting five to six hours of sleep on several nights per week. Notice I said *several* nights and not *every* night, for I found that if I got at least one solid night of eight hours sleep per week, I could get by on less sleep for the rest of the week. Saying that I was "getting by" on five to six hours of sleep also is an admission that this was not ideal, but it was necessary under the circumstances. Your own sleep patterns may have to balance the demands of what your body ideally needs with the demands placed on your time by the responsibilities of work, school, and family.

There is no doubt that an improper amount of sleep will adversely affect your performance, and this isn't only for running. It is always crucial to get a good night's sleep before doing anything for which we are expected or hoping to perform at our best, such as taking a test, going for a job interview, or running a marathon. Because many people are nervous and, as a result, sleep fitfully the night before a big event, sometimes it is better to focus on getting a good night's sleep *two* nights before the big event.

The Use of Caffeine

Any discussion of sleep should also include the topic of caffeine. I mentioned in a previous chapter that I gave up caffeine in 1989 and I have been basically caffeine-free ever since. For me, being caffeine-free means avoiding anything with caffeine in it, including chocolate and colas. When I decline chocolates that are offered to me, people ask, "You don't like chocolate?" To which I respond, "I love chocolate, but I can't eat it because chocolate has caffeine." I will admit that I'll have an occasional chocolate chip cookie or chocolate chip ice cream, but the caffeine level of the amount of chocolate in those items is so small that it usually does not bother me.

Why did I give up caffeine? I was never a big coffee drinker and I rarely drank more than a cup or two of coffee in the morning. Eventually I discovered that my body was very sensitive to even relatively small amounts of caffeine. While my father could drink a cup of regular coffee right before going to bed and fall fast asleep, I did not get that disposition. I first noticed when I was in college that if I had a cola or two in the evening, I would toss and turn for quite a while before eventually falling asleep, even if I was tired and had stayed up late.

The factor that most persuaded me to give up caffeine was when I discovered that I would get a severe caffeine-withdrawal headache by noon if I did not have a cup of coffee in the morning. Because having a cup or two of coffee in the morning was part of my daily routine, I only discovered this when the routine was interrupted. Ironically, and perhaps providentially, the catalyst for this was going for my annual medical exam. Because the physical usually included routine blood tests, the doctor would give instructions not to eat or drink anything other than water on the day of the physical. Invariably, on returning home, I would have a splitting headache. At first, I wondered why visiting the doctor would give me a headache, until I realized that it wasn't the doctor giving me a headache, but the lack of caffeine on that day.

I ultimately made the decision to quit caffeine after spending six weeks studying Polish language and culture in Poland during the summer of 1989. The pastor who hosted me that summer at his parish rectory in Lublin was very hospitable, as were the Polish people in general. Of course, Polish hospitality included serving large amounts of coffee and tea, often in a tall tumbler with the coffee grounds at the bottom of the glass. Not surprisingly, I finished my time in Poland feeling that my nervous system was laced with caffeine from too many cups of espresso, cappuccino, coffee, and tea. The clincher was that I was then scheduled for my annual physical shortly afterward. I decided that I would plan ahead to avoid the splitting headache that came with these doctor's visits, so I gradually weaned myself off caffeine over several days, at first with a blend of three-fourths regular coffee and one-fourth decaffeinated coffee, then half and half, then three-fourths decaf and one-fourth regular coffee, until eventually I was drinking only decaf coffee. The weaning process did involve some mild headaches, but I did successfully avoid the usual acute, throbbing headache on the day of my physical exam. That's when I decided I was not going back to being dependent on caffeine.

Now, I realize that some 90 percent of people drink coffee, so I am not going to try to persuade everyone to give up their lattes and espressos. If you can consume caffeine without adverse effects or dependency, you're lucky, but even then you should realize that caffeine is a drug and, for some, an addictive drug at that. Caffeine affects the brain to make people feel more alert and less tired. In some ways it is also a performance-enhancing drug. That's why some packets of energy gels contain caffeine and runners pop them along the marathon course. Using caffeine is not illegal, but I prefer to use my natural energy and not rely on using a stimulant to enhance my performance.

As a stimulant, caffeine also works to mask fatigue. When driving for a long stretch, for example, motorists will often have a cup of coffee, a cola, or an energy drink to help keep them awake. The problem with masking fatigue on a regular basis is that you begin to fool your mind that your body is less tired than it really is. While caffeine often provides a short-term boost, eventually its effects wear off and our bodies become more tolerant, thus needing to consume ever greater quantities to feel the same effect. This is not helpful for improving performance in the long run (pun intended).

In practice, for me this means that when I am feeling tired, my body is giving me a signal that it needs more rest. Rather than masking that warning from my body with a cup of coffee to make me feel less tired, I take it as a sign that I need to get to bed earlier that night and get more sleep. Then, after a good night's sleep, I wake up the next morning feeling rested and refreshed, ready for my run and the day ahead of me.

Nutrition, Fasting, and Abstinence

The topic of whether or not to use caffeine leads to the area of nutrition in general. What should a runner eat and drink to achieve peak performance? Indeed, what should anyone eat and drink to be physically *and* spiritually healthy? You may understand the obvious connection between nutrition and physical health but be less clear about what eating and drinking have to do with your spiritual life. You need look no further than the ascetical practices of fasting and abstaining from certain foods and drinks at particular times and occasions to see the connection with spiritual practices that people have observed over the centuries.

When I was growing up in the early 1960s, before the Second Vatican Council, I remember the strict obligation that required Catholics to abstain from meat every Friday throughout the year. Sometimes that was a severe penance for me, but other times it was not. Mom frequently cooked delicious meatless dinners that I looked forward to eating, such as potato pancakes, egg salad, and her own miniature homemade pizzas that she made with English muffins, topped with tomatoes and mozzarella cheese. Every few weeks, however, Mom would cook breaded fish sticks. I hated them! Mom's cooking was great, so it wasn't her fault. I just could not stomach the fishy taste. Mom had a rule, though, that my siblings and I had to eat everything she put on our plate, or we would have to spend the rest of the evening in our room. I spent many a

Friday night in solitary confinement. Either way, whether it was eating fish or being confined to my room, Fridays were often a day of real penance for me.

While Good Friday and Ash Wednesday continue to be days of fasting and abstinence and all the Fridays of Lent are still to be maintained as days of abstinence from meat, what many people seem not to know is that *every* Friday is still to be a day of penance for Catholics. When Pope St. Paul VI changed the rules and said that abstaining from meat every Friday was no longer required, he emphasized that abstaining from meat was supposed to be done as a penance, but in some cases it clearly was not, such as when a person would choose an expensive delicacy like lobster to eat instead of meat.

In the cases when abstaining from meat is not a penance, some other penance should be done to substitute, such as volunteer work in hospitals, visiting the sick, serving the needs of the aged and the lonely, instructing the young in the faith. We do penance on Fridays because Jesus died on the cross to save us from our sins on Good Friday, so Friday should always be a day of penance.

Fasting before Communion

The Church also instructs Catholics in another form of fasting. Before 1964, Catholics were also required to fast from all food and drink (except water and medicine) from midnight on the night before going to Mass until receiving Holy Communion. Now, canon 919 of the *Code of Canon Law* states, "One who is to receive the Most Holy Eucharist is to abstain from any food or drink, with the exception of water and medicine, for at least the period of one hour before Holy Communion." There are two exceptions to this rule. First, a priest who celebrates Mass two or three times on the same day may eat or drink something before the second or third celebration even if there is less than one hour in between. This allows him to maintain strength when he needs to celebrate more than one Mass that day. Second, those who are advanced in age or who suffer from any infirmity, as well as those who take care of them, can receive the holy Eucharist even if they have taken food or drink during the previous hour.

Knowing the rules is one thing; knowing why we have these rules is another. Practices like fasting and abstinence have more meaning for us if we know the reasons behind them.

Fasting is a form of *mortification*, which comes from the Latin word *mors*, which means "death." Mortification involves dying to our own desires in order to identify with the death of Jesus and thus free ourselves from being slaves of our own passions. Pope St. Paul VI once explained mortification of the flesh as "clearly revealed if we consider the fragility of our nature, in which, since Adam's sin, flesh and spirit have contrasting desires." While the exercise of bodily mortification should not be understood to imply a condemnation of the flesh in which God created us, mortification aims to liberate us from the chains of our own senses. Through bodily fasting, we regain spiritual strength and the wound of our fallen nature is cured by the medicine of a wholesome abstinence.

St. Paul described this dying to oneself in his second letter to the Corinthians, saying that we Christians are "always carrying about in the body the dying of Jesus, so that the life of Jesus may also be manifested in our body. For we who live are constantly being given up to death for the sake of Jesus, so that the life of Jesus may be manifested in our mortal flesh" (4:10–11).

Practically all religions have some form of fasting and abstinence. Muslims, for example, are expected to abstain from food and drink between sunrise and sunset for thirty days during *Ramadan*, the ninth month of the Islamic calendar. The Tibetan Buddhist practice of *Nyungne* ("nyoong-nay") is a profound, two-and-a-half-day keeping of strict vows, complete silence and fasting. Participants say the practice purifies them both physically and spiritually. Hindus fast on certain days of the month such as *Purnima* (full moon) and *Ekadasi* (the eleventh day of the fortnight), on certain days of the week, and on festivals. Some Hindus do not eat meat on certain days and other Hindus do not eat meat at all. The Jewish calendar contains several fast days, which involve abstaining from food and drink from dawn until dark, most of them commemorating various landmark events that revolve around the destruction of the Holy Temples. *Yom Kippur* ("Day of Atonement"), the holiest day of the Jewish calendar, has its own rules for fasting.

The New Testament has several mentions of fasting. St. John the Baptist, considered the prophet who bridged the Old Testament and New Testament, and his disciples fasted (cf. Mt 9:14; Mk 2:19; Lk 5:33). St. Paul also explicitly linked discipline, such as fasting, to training your body to run a race: "Do you not know that the runners in the stadium all run in the race, but only one wins the prize? Run so as to win. Every athlete exercises discipline in every way. They do it to win a perishable crown, but we an imperishable one. Thus I do not run aimlessly; I do not fight as if I were shadowboxing. No, I drive my body and train it, for fear that, after having preached to others, I myself should be disqualified" (1 Cor 9:24–27).

When I was training for my Boston-qualifying marathon, I gave up eating meat and drinking alcohol (except for the small amount of sacramental wine used at Mass), focusing on a high-carbohydrate, low-protein diet. That meant a lot of pasta, fruit, and vegetables. It was not a strictly vegan diet, as I would eat eggs, cheese, and even some fish to make sure I was getting protein. Peanut butter is also a good source of protein, which I love to spread on apples, pears, bananas, and other fruit. This high-carbohydrate, low-protein, no-alcohol diet worked for me and I qualified for the Boston Marathon.

I am not a nutritionist, but we did have a nutritionist speak to us at a workshop as part of the Chicago Area Runners Association Marathon Training Program. I remember the nutritionist explaining why carbo-loading is recommended for runners. She said that during high-endurance exercise, like running, biking, and swimming, the body burns glycogen, and glycogen comes from carbohydrates. While protein is needed to rebuild muscles, carbohydrates give our muscles fuel to burn. The nutritionist said that we store glycogen in our muscles and in our liver, and that our muscles and liver have the capacity to store enough glycogen for us to run about twenty miles. That explains why many marathon runners "hit the wall" between miles twenty and twenty-six, basically because we have burned out our glycogen. At that point, all kinds of red alerts and alarms are going off in our brains, commanding us to stop whatever we're doing because we have burned out our fuel.

Of course, marathon runners do not stop running when they hit the wall, otherwise they would not finish and would never be considered a marathon runner! This is not just a matter of gutting it out, as there are some things that we can do to lessen the severity of hitting the wall. The most basic remedy is simply to refuel along the way. It is important to stay hydrated with water and energy drinks at the water stations provided at regular intervals, usually about every mile and a half or two miles. Even if you don't feel thirsty, your body will need the hydration and the electrolytes of the energy drinks while running a marathon.

Eating along the way is a bit more challenging. I recommend experimenting with trying to eat something during your training runs rather than trying to eat for the first time during a marathon. This way you can find out what works and what doesn't work. For example, I tried taking along some peaches once on a training run, thinking they would be fairly soft and easy to digest. So I put a couple of peaches in a pouch in my waist belt. After a few miles when I thought I would have a peach, I opened the pouch and found a mush of peach juice!

If you want to eat some fruit along the way, I found that a banana works pretty well. The skin help to keep the fruit from turning to mush from bouncing and shaking in your pocket or waist pouch. An orange also has a protective skin, but it is much harder to peel than a banana. While taking a break to peel your orange on a training run might work, it's probably not a good idea to try that while running a marathon unless you really don't care about your finish time and are willing to take a more extended break somewhere along the way as you peel your orange. Fortunately, some race organizers or just plain friendly people in front of their houses along the way occasionally offer pieces of oranges and bananas already peeled that you can just grab as you run by. But don't forget to say thank you!

Then there is the question of energy bars. I usually don't like to eat too much before a training run or the marathon itself, as I don't like a lot of food bouncing in my stomach. Some fuel for the run is needed, however, so I have found that an energy bar and some juice are about all I need to get started. Eating energy bars along the way is an entirely a different matter. I have tried doing so and it is possible, but it is hard to run and chew at the same time if you are trying to eat on the run (literally) without stopping. It's not that I am too uncoordinated to run and chew at the same time, but the bigger challenge is chewing and breathing at the same time, especially if you're moving at a good clip. Obviously, you need to keep inhaling and exhaling as you're running, and it's hard to do that efficiently if your mouth is full of food.

The best solution I found is to consume energy gels instead of energy bars. There are different brands, such as Power Gel and Gu, that come filled with healthy nutrients in different flavors wrapped in individual packets that you can stuff in your pockets and pop along the way. Note that some gel packs come loaded with caffeine, so you might want to check the label if you have given up caffeine, as I have. In my experience of running marathons, I have found that one packet of energy gel every forty-five minutes or so helps me to replenish my fuel reserves and stave off hitting the wall between mile twenty and the finish. This is usually best done right before approaching a water station so you can wash down the gel with some water or energy drink.

Another helpful tip that I picked up some years ago was to take along a small piece of peppermint candy, like the kind that you get as a breath freshener wrapped in cellophane when you're leaving a restaurant. I always put one in my pocket and pop one of those into my mouth at about mile twenty-four. The sugar goes right to your brain and helps you to get over the wall in the last stretch of the marathon!

Pain Management

Rest is the remedy that is often prescribed for pain. Rest is not always a practical option, however, given our responsibilities and commitments. Life is filled with difficulties and our bodies experience a variety of discomforts, aches, and pains on a daily basis. Athletes of all sorts (and perhaps runners especially) know the feeling of sore muscles and tired ligaments after putting in a strenuous workout. Athletes who give in too easily to minor aches and pains are not going to make much progress in their training. That's where the saying comes from: "no pain, no gain!"

That is also why we have coaches. Coaches show us techniques and the mechanics of the sports we play, but they also help to motivate us and push us to greater effort and exertion when we're feeling lethargic or perhaps just plain lazy. The trick is to know when the pain is a hurdle to overcome and when it is a signal to stop. God created us to experience pain as a way to alert us that something is wrong. It takes careful discernment of the cause of the pain and calculation of the severity of the discomfort to know whether to stop and rest from exercise or simply to push through it.

I'll tell you a story from my personal experience to illustrate what I mean. On October 24, 1999, I ran and completed the Chicago Marathon in three hours and thirty-six minutes. Then, I decided to run the Rome Marathon on January 1, 2000. The Rome Marathon is usually run in the spring, but in 2000 the marathon officials scheduled it for New Year's Day as a way to mark the beginning of the new millennium. They called it the *Maratona del Giubileo*, Italian for "Marathon of the Jubilee," in honor of the celebration of the third millennium of Christianity. I figured running a marathon was a pretty cool way to start a new millennium, so I signed up.

The challenge that this presented was balancing the rest I needed after the Chicago Marathon in October and the training I would need to do to be ready for the Rome Marathon just a few weeks later. After giving myself what I thought was enough rest after the Chicago Marathon, I resumed training with a more accelerated program of increased mileage than I would usually do over an eighteen-week marathon training program. Sure enough, it was not exactly a surprise when I developed a sore left ankle in early December.

I went to see my friend, Dr. Brian Macaulay, a marathon runner, who at the time was working as an emergency room physician at Norwegian American Hospital on the north side of Chicago. I was worried that perhaps I had incurred a stress fracture as a result of overtraining. After taking an X-ray of my ankle, Dr. Macaulay said that there was no sign of any stress fracture nor could he see anything else that might be causing my pain. So I asked him what I should do.

Dr. Macaulay replied, "As your physician, I would advise you to rest your ankle until it feels better."

I said, "Brian, I came to you not only because you are a doctor, but also because you are a marathon runner. The Rome Marathon is just two weeks away. If you were in my position, what would you do?"

He replied, "Oh, what would *I* do?"

"Yes, what would *you* do?" I asked again.

He answered, "Well, I guess I would tape my ankle, take some ibuprofen, and run the marathon."

So that is exactly what I did! It was somewhat painful and not easy running on the cobblestoned streets of Rome, but I finished in four hours and thirty-two minutes, almost an hour slower than my prior marathon just a few weeks previously. The important thing is that I finished. The marathon started in St. Peter's Square after Pope St. John Paul II's blessing of the runners at the noon Angelus, so I finished the winter marathon after sunset. My photo at the finish line shows a darkened Colosseum in the background.

My point is that sometimes we can run through pain, but too much pain means we should stop and let the painful area rest and heal. My default mode is to try to run through the pain. More often than not, it works for me and eventually the pain goes away. I get plenty of soreness in my ankles, knees, hips, lower back, and neck. I have had plantar fasciitis, the name for the condition that develops when that tissue becomes inflamed. It is the bane of many runners because it involves a painful heel caused by a strain and inflammation of the tissue that connects the heel bone to the toes. When the plantar fascia is excessively stretched, micro-tears can occur, causing this swelling and subsequent pain. This usually can take up to six months to heal.

My worst and most painful injury was a herniated disc in the C5-6 vertebrae of my upper spine in my neck. I am not 100 percent sure, but I think it was caused when I slipped and fell while running on icy pavement one winter morning in Chicago. The temperature was about 32 degrees and there was ice and snow on the ground. I knew that would be hazardous but I had run before many times in those conditions and thought that I would just do a short run while being careful.

Well, it turned out to be a very short run! I went no more than a half block when I slipped on a patch of ice I didn't see and my feet went out from under me, landing me face first on the sidewalk. I picked myself up, touched my forehead where it had hit the ground, and saw that my glove was bloody. So I walked back to the rectory, feeling a bit dizzy. Fortunately, the pastor of the parish was home and drove me to the emergency room. I was lying on the examining table when a nurse handed me a piece of gauze and told me to cover my right eye with it, explaining that she was going to glue the wound shut on my forehead instead of using stitches. The glue was like super glue and she wanted to make sure she didn't glue my eyelid shut. At the time, I was diagnosed with nothing more than a slight concussion.

Within a couple of weeks, however, I was experiencing the most excruciating pain in my neck, radiating from my spine along my right arm to the tip of my right index finger. I went to my primary physician who ordered some tests, the results of which showed I had a herniated disc in the C5-6 vertebrae of my upper spine in my neck. The doctor recommended a conservative approach since such herniated discs often heal themselves over time. I asked what would happen if it didn't heal by itself. He said in that case he would refer me to a neurosurgeon or an orthopedic surgeon. I didn't like hearing about options that mentioned surgery, so I decided to visit my chiropractor.

I went to see a chiropractor named Dr. Alden Clendenin, a fellow hockey player whom I had met at the ice rink. He was also the team chiropractor for the Chicago Cubs. Initially I had so much pain that he couldn't touch me, so he sent me to a pain doctor who gave me an epidural. Then I was able to see Dr. Clendenin five days per week for a couple of weeks initially, and then we scaled back the visits to twice a week, then twice a month, as I started to improve. His adjustments to my neck and manipulations of my bones and muscles definitely helped to the point where I was able to resume running and playing hockey. Finally, we settled on a once per month schedule, mainly just for maintenance. This experience made me a firm believer in the benefits of chiropractic medicine.

Whether or not you should try to run through an injury, or rest the injury, or see a doctor, depends on your tolerance for pain. There is no simple answer as people have different pain thresholds and the choice of what to do will depend on the severity of the injury. In case of doubt, don't try to be a hero, but go see your doctor.

Posture and Stretching

Preventing injuries and running more efficiently can also be helped by running with good posture, namely, keeping your head held upright, your back straight, and your arms held low at your side. In contrast, the tendency of many runners, especially when fatigued, is to run with head bowed, back hunched over, and arms pumping high near your neck. Running this way compresses your lungs and causes you to breathe less efficiently, adding to your fatigue. A more upright posture helps your lungs to expand to full capacity and get more oxygen to your muscles.

In addition to running with good posture, it is important to stretch both before and after running, especially as you get older. Running tends to tighten muscles, so it is important to work to keep them loose. There are all kinds of stretching exercises, like toe touches, hamstring stretches, hip flexor stretches, knee to chest stretches, quad stretches, and neck stretches. I won't go into describing those here, as you can find plenty of websites and online videos that demonstrate these stretches for you. The important point I want to make is to do them, and make sure you're doing them slowly and deliberately, not with a sharp or jerky motion. This will help to increase your flexibility and improve the efficiency of your running motion.

Shoes and Running Apparel

Last but not least for this chapter is a word about shoes and other running apparel. Running is a rather inexpensive sport. Your main expenses will be for good shoes, proper running apparel, and your race registration fees. When it comes to shoes, I strongly advise that you don't go cheap and skimp. Your feet take a lot of pounding in training and running marathons, so you should make sure your shoes provide proper fit, cushion, and support. There are some people that swear by barefoot running, but they are distinctly in the minority and I am not one of them. Without the good running shoes and the custom-made orthotics I wear in them to support my fallen arches, I am sure that I would never have been able to do as much running as I have without serious injury for so many years.

In terms of finding which shoe is best for you, a good place to start is the shoe guide and shoe review in *Runners World* (which can be found online). There you will find descriptions and analyses of various brands and types or running shoes to match your specific needs. I also highly recommend going to a store that specializes in selling running shoes. The salespeople there have often worked with many different types of runners with various physiques.

Some of them will even have you get on a treadmill to analyze your running gait and determine if you need to adjust for over pronation or under pronation. Pronation is the natural side-to-side movement of your feet as you walk or run. If you over pronate, your foot rolls inward (common in people with flatter feet), so you would need a stability shoe to help evenly distribute the impact. If you under pronate (also known as a supinator or supination), your foot rolls outward (common in people with high arches), and you would need a shoe with extra cushioning or features to control the motion to absorb the impact. Oftentimes, the shoe salesperson can tell if you over pronate or under pronate just by watching you run for a bit.

I have found over the years that it is a good idea to buy running shoes that are a full size to a size and a half larger than your everyday street shoes. My street shoe is a size eleven, while I wear a size twelve-and-a-half running shoe. The reason is that your feet swell as you run, and the swelling of your feet will have your toes pounding against the front of your shoe for an extended time on a long training run or in running a marathon. This will cause your toenails to blacken and eventually fall off. That has happened to me a few times. It's not a big problem as your toenails will grow back in a few months, but it doesn't make for nice-looking feet! Larger running shoes will help prevent that. A good test when you're at the shoe store trying on your running shoes is that you should be able to press down about the width of your thumb on the front of the shoe between your big toe and the tip of the shoe.

In terms of running apparel, you want to stay away from 100 percent cotton clothing, which absorbs and retains the moisture of your sweat, and instead use materials that wick the moisture away. You also need to dress according to the temperature. I do not like running on a treadmill, so I usually run outdoors even when it is very cold, and I keep warm simply by adding layers depending on the temperature. You also need to remember that you will generate heat from your own body as you are running. After years of running, I have a pretty good feel for how I need to dress depending on the weather. Beginning runners tend to dress too warmly as they start out. If you go out for a run in the cold and are dressed in such a way that you feel warm before you have even started running, you're probably overdressed, since after a half mile or so the heat from your body will warm you. The advantage of dressing in layers as opposed to wearing a heavy coat is that you can always take off a layer if you feel too warm and either carry it in your hand or tie the sleeves around your waist.

Although I will sometimes wear gloves if the temperature is sub-freezing, I find that my hands quickly warm up once I get going and I either put the gloves in my pocket or just wind up carrying the gloves in my hand. If the temperature is below 0 degrees Fahrenheit, I wear a scarf to cover my mouth and most of my face. (I told you I run outside in most conditions!) With a stocking cap over the top of my head and ears, only my eyes are left uncovered. Even in such cold, I still sweat when I run, so the main effect is that icicles start to form on my eyelashes. Otherwise, running in the cold does not pose much of a problem for me. Maybe as a hockey player I'm just used to exercising in the freezing cold!

Finally, if you have fair skin like I do, you should wear sunscreen and a hat. In my marathon photos, I am always wearing my trusty White Sox baseball cap!

In this chapter, we have looked at various ways to relax, rest, recover, replenish, refresh, repair, and renew our bodies and our souls. In the next chapter, we will discuss the rewards that come from spiritual and physical wellness.

Quotation

"You have made us for yourself, O Lord, and our heart is restless until it rests in you."

—St. Augustine, *Confessions*

Promise

I promise to balance hard work with rest, to allow the Lord to refresh my body and restore my soul.

Prayer

O God, as you rested after your work of creation, help us to keep holy our Sabbath repose so that we may rest in you. Give us the graces we need to restore the strength and vigor of our bodies when we are fatigued and renew the enthusiasm of our spirits when our zeal begins to wane. We ask this through Christ our Lord. Amen.

7.

Reward

Achieving our physical and spiritual goals brings a great sense of personal satisfaction and reward.

Running is a good illustration of the saying "A virtue is its own reward." The act of running every day is virtuous as both a means and an end. As a means, running helps us to stay healthy. But running itself has its own joys and rewards, separate and apart from the goal of staying healthy.

For example, you may know of the story of Eric Liddell, a devout Christian, who won the men's 400-meter running competition at the 1924 Olympics in Paris, France. Eric was depicted in the movie *Chariots of Fire* which includes his famous line: "I believe that God made me for a purpose, but he also made me fast. When I run, I feel his pleasure." To say that virtue is its own reward means that living a virtuous life is not just a means to an end but is worth doing just for the sake of doing it.

What is a virtue? A virtue is a good habit. Oppositely, a vice is a bad habit. Habits of both kinds are repeated actions. We want to foster the virtues as repeated, good habits, and avoid vices as repeated, bad habits. The *Catechism of the Catholic Church* explains that being virtuous "allows the person not only to perform good acts, but to give the best of himself. The virtuous person tends toward the good with all his sensory and spiritual powers; he pursues the good and chooses it in concrete actions" (1803). St. Gregory of Nyssa wrote in the fourth century that "the goal of a virtuous life is to become like God."

Just as we need good training habits to be good runners, we need good habits for daily living to become saints. In chapter 2, I wrote that the concept of being a canonized saint should not be understood as some remote idea from centuries ago but should be a real goal that we see as within our reach. Think of the virtues as good habits for everyday life that can help you to reach the goal of sainthood. These good habits need not be profound gestures, but often are simply small and even unnoticed acts that can be done on a daily basis.

Overcoming Vices with Virtues

A vice, that is, a bad habit, can be countered with virtues. One example of how this is so comes from a societal vice I notice while on my runs. Perhaps it is just my imagination, but the problem of litter seems to be getting worse in recent years. After my morning runs, I usually cool down by walking around the grounds of our cathedral. In recent months I have noticed what seems to be an increased amount of trash apparently thrown out of car windows by passersby, including empty beer cans, soda cups, pizza boxes, hamburger containers, banana peels, and more.

This disheartens me. I am old enough to remember the public service announcements that ran on American television fifty or so years ago with the slogan "Don't be a litterbug." The anti-litter campaign was promoted by an organization called Keep America Beautiful, founded in 1953 in response to the growing problem of highway litter. Because I think this is unsightly for people coming to Mass and since I am often out there early before our maintenance worker can get to it, I pick it up myself.

Once, I was picking up the litter in front of the cathedral as a woman came out of the church. I was wearing my running clothes and my customary Sox baseball cap. She asked me if I worked there. I said yes, whereupon she directed me to the corner of the lawn in front of our rectory next to the cathedral with the instruction that I should pick up the dog droppings there. I said I would take care of it right away! Afterward, I thought it appropriate that the bishop should be mistaken for the gardener!

It is true that a bad habit, like littering, can be countered by a virtue, a good habit, such as cleanliness. The litterbug says, "The world is my garbage can and so I am free to throw my trash wherever I want." Never mind the unsightly effect this has on the environment or the inconvenience imposed on others who have to pick up the other person's trash. In this sense vices are vicious, as the offender seeks only to do as he or she pleases regardless of whether it is displeasing to others. In contrast, the virtuous person seeks to please God and make life more pleasant for others.

Christ Is the Way, the Truth, and the Life

The reward of living a virtuous life in Jesus Christ is indeed sainthood. This is the ultimate goal of our lives on earth. How do we achieve this? In his multi-volume work , *In Conversation with God*, Fr. Francis Fernandez writes that "We must start by making the desire for holiness flourish in our own soul, telling our Lord: 'I want to be a saint'; or at least, 'When I experience my softness and weakness, I *want* to want to be a saint.' To banish doubt and make holiness more than an empty word let us turn and look at Christ." The invitation to "look at Christ" reminds me of one of my favorite passages in the Bible, from the letter to the Hebrews:

> Therefore, since we are surrounded by so great a cloud of witnesses, let us rid ourselves of every burden and sin that clings to us and persevere in running the race that lies before us, fixing our eyes on Jesus, the author and perfecter of faith. For the sake of the joy that lay before him he endured the cross, despising its shame, and has taken his seat at the right hand of the throne of God. (12:1–2)

There are several significant aspects of this scripture passage that resonate with me. First, as a marathon runner, I can certainly relate to the need to persevere in "running the race that lies before us" in a literal sense. But I can also relate to this instruction in a metaphorical sense. We run a spiritual race to our ultimate goal, the reward of eternal life, by "fixing our eyes on Jesus." Why is it so important to keep Jesus in our sight? The answer is found in the Bible verse that you often see someone holding up on a sign at a sporting event or at a parade—John 3:16—that says, "For God so loved the world that he gave his only Son, so that everyone who believes in him might not perish but might have eternal life." The reason we fix our eyes on Jesus is that he is our way to heaven. Jesus also said, "I am the way and the truth and the life. No one comes to the Father except through me" (Jn 14:6).

Also, as I shared in chapter 5, to persevere on our path to holiness, we must not only keep our eyes fixed on Jesus, we must also work on having a loving relationship with Jesus and making him the center of our lives. I would add here that there are several different ways of relating to Jesus, for example, he is Lord and Savior as well as our friend, and brother.

The Holy Name of Jesus Christ

To unpack these types of relationships, let's start with the Holy Name: Jesus Christ. The name "Jesus" comes from the Hebrew and Aramaic name *Yeshua*, which in English is sometimes rendered as Joshua. The name *Yeshua* means "YHWH [the Lord] is salvation." This name is alluded to in the Gospels where an angel of the Lord appears to Joseph in a dream and tells him that Mary "will bear a son and you are to name him Jesus, because he will save his people from their sins" (Mt 1:21; see also Lk 2:21).

The name "Christ" comes from the Greek *Christos*, which translates as "the Anointed One" and is translated in Hebrew as *Messiah*. Jesus had identified himself as the Messiah after being anointed by the Holy Spirit while reading from the scroll of the prophet Isaiah in his hometown synagogue in Nazareth (see Luke 14:4–30). By this name, Christians profess their belief that Jesus is the Messiah, as St. Peter said in response to Jesus' question, "Who do you say that I am?" Peter exclaimed in reply, "You are the Messiah, the Son of the living God" (Mt 16:15–16). Jesus asks each of us the same question with the desire that in faith we will respond in the same way as Peter.

Taken literally, then, the name of Jesus Christ means "the Lord, our Salvation, the Anointed One." It is from this name that we get our identity as *Christ*ians since we are incorporated into the Body of Christ when we are baptized. In the Catholic Church, each one of us is also anointed with the sacred chrism, holy oil that symbolizes the Holy Spirit, right after we are washed in the saving waters of Baptism. We are anointed again in the Sacrament of Confirmation when we are fully initiated into the Church and receive the fullness of the Holy Spirit. Every priest and bishop is additionally an *alter Christus*—another Christ—because in the Sacrament of Holy Orders the palms of the priest's hands are anointed with the sacred chrism, whereby he is configured to Christ in a special way. In the rite of ordination for bishops, the head of the bishop is anointed with the sacred chrism to show the outpouring of the Holy Spirit upon him. He serves as the vicar of Christ in his diocese.

Do You Accept Jesus as Your Lord and Savior?

I have been asked by some evangelical Christians—once while wearing my clerical collar as I was visiting the sick in a hospital—whether I "accepted Jesus Christ as my Lord and Savior." As a baptized Catholic, my answer is always, "Yes, of course!" Some may see the formal declaration of "accepting Jesus Christ as my personal Lord and Savior" as one used more by evangelical Protestants than by Catholics. While evangelical Protestants and Catholics may have different understandings of the implications of this phrase, no one group of Christians has a copyright on it! In fact, it is not only acceptable, but it is even essential for Catholics as much as for Protestants to accept Jesus Christ as their Lord and Savior.

The reference to Jesus Christ as our Lord and Savior is quite biblical. In the Acts of the Apostles, St. Peter is quoted saying of Jesus: "There is no salvation through anyone else, nor is there any other name under heaven given to the human race by which we are to be saved" (Acts 4:12). Similarly, St. Paul wrote in his letter to the Romans: "For if you confess with your mouth that Jesus is Lord and believe in your heart that God raised him from the dead, you will be saved. . . . For everyone who calls on the name of the Lord will be saved" (Romans 10:9, 13).

Protestants often refer to accepting Jesus Christ as their Lord and Savior as being "born again." Catholic theology teaches that we are born again spiritually at Baptism (cf. Jn

3:5). Nevertheless, Catholics must also at some point in their lives make a conscious and deliberate decision to accept Jesus as their Lord and Savior, no matter what the cost to them. This deliberate decision will be strengthened and reinforced if we consciously reaffirm it every time that we recite the Creed, renew our baptismal promises, and receive Holy Communion. The *Catechism of the Catholic Church* calls our conscious and deliberate decision to accept Jesus Christ as Lord and Savior a second conversion: "This second conversion is an uninterrupted task for the whole Church" (1428).

In other words, conversion to Christ is a lifelong process, but it must start sometime. For some, that may indeed be the moment of their Baptism. For others, it may come upon receiving the Sacrament of Confirmation, or during a high school retreat, or on a Cursillo weekend, upon entering marriage, or the birth of children, in the face of serious illness, or the death of a loved one. The point is that all Catholics must at some time make it their own choice to accept Jesus Christ as Lord and Savior and to make him the Master of their lives.

A good example of what this means was illustrated in a conversation I had with a man who met up with me as part of our diocesan synod on discipleship and evangelization in 2017. A diocesan synod is an official meeting between clergy and laity. This was the fourth synod in the history of the Diocese of Springfield. The man explained that he had been challenged by an evangelical Christian friend as to whether he truly accepted Jesus as his Lord and Savior. He told me that although he went to Mass every Sunday, contributed financially to the support of his parish, and lived according to the moral teachings of the Church, he had to admit that he had not placed Christ above everyone and everything else in his life. I wondered what he was placing in front of Christ in his life. In fact, he explained, it was not a *what* but a *who*. He told me that he loved his wife so much that he loved her above Jesus. We talked and I explained the problem with putting a spouse in front of God is that we then expect the spouse to be perfect when, in fact, they can't be. This can lead to marital problems when expectations are not met. The man admitted his relationship with his wife was indeed going through difficult times. The solution for him was to make Jesus Christ the sovereign Master and Lord of his life, to put his relationship with his wife into that proper perspective. He could still love his wife intensely, but only secondarily to his love for God.

Thus, being a disciple of our Lord means putting Christ at the center of your life, in the very depths your heart, and living in such a way that reflects the fact that Jesus is your sovereign Master. The Catholic understanding of being a disciple of Jesus Christ also recognizes that there is a Church dimension to discipleship. In other words, we are committed to living a Christian life *within* the Catholic Church. The Christian way of life is not a personal philosophy or a self-centered journey; it is a journey of faith with the community of believers travelling together on the path to heaven.

Facing Obstacles on the Way

Just as getting to the finish line of a marathon has its challenges and hurdles to overcome, the path to heaven is laced with many obstacles as well. The passage from the letter to the Hebrews (p. 120) that speaks of ridding ourselves of burden and sin alludes to these obstacles.

Burdens come in many forms. For example, once while in Dallas, I decided to go out for a training run. I had driven my car to the Trinity River and then planned to run three miles along one bank, cross a bridge over the river, and then run back on the other side. It was a typical brutally hot day in Texas. What I didn't know was that it had rained the day before and the banks of the river were muddy. As I ran, the mud began caking up on the bottom of my running shoes. By the time I reached the halfway point at the bridge, the mud on my shoes was so thick that it felt like I had lead weights in my shoes. I thought the run back to my car was going to be really tough, but the other bank of the river was on higher ground and was not so muddy, so I stopped to see if I could scrape the mud off my shoes. To my amazement, the layer of mud easily peeled off each shoe in one piece! I was able to run back in a normal fashion, feeling much lighter on my feet.

A few hours after my run, when I was praying, it struck me that the letter to the Hebrews described it perfectly: "Let us rid ourselves of every burden and sin that clings to us and persevere in running." My prayer that day reflected on how sin weighs us down and makes life so difficult to keep going. When we go to confession and receive God's forgiveness, it is like peeling off a layer of mud from the bottom of our shoes. When freed by God's merciful love, we are released from the burden of sin and can persevere in running the course of our lives toward our goal with our eyes fixed on Jesus: life on high with Christ in God's kingdom!

Overcoming the Obstacles of Vices with Virtues

Since virtues are good habits, they can make life less complicated for us if we practice them, because if our virtuous habits come naturally, we hardly need to give much thought as to what to do next in many routine situations. Unfortunately, however, since vices are bad habits, we can fall into the trap of engaging in bad behaviors routinely as well. The remedy is to foster virtues as an antidote to vices.

As a runner, I described earlier how I like to start my day with praying while running. You could say, in a sense, that this is a virtuous way of living since it starts each day with a good habit. It also overcomes the vice of laziness or sloth. Even though I might prefer to stay in bed and sleep longer, my good habit of getting up and going out the door with my finger rosary to run and pray helps me to overcome the tendency to lethargy. It is not a sin if you don't go running on any given day, but it is also not virtuous if you let yourself slide into a pattern of laziness and inertia. At the same time, living a virtuous life does help to overcome temptations for us to do things that are, in fact, sinful.

You may have heard of the *seven deadly sins*, sometimes referred to as the "seven mortal sins," "seven capital sins" or "seven capital vices." Mortal sins are deadly because they kill our relationship with God due to their seriousness. The Latin word for capital, *capitalis*, refers to the head or source of life; thus, "capital punishment" is a name for the death penalty. St. Thomas Aquinas said that the seven capital sins are deadly because they lead to many other sins. We read, for example, how King David's adultery with Bathsheba led to the sin of murder when he ordered that Bathsheba's husband be killed (see 2 Sm 11:1–27).

The seven deadly sins are pride, envy, anger, avarice, gluttony, lust, and sloth. Each of these deadly vices has a remedy in at least one of the virtues:

- The remedy for pride is the virtue of humility.
- The remedy for envy is the virtue of gratitude for the gifts you have received from God.
- The remedy for anger is the virtue of meekness or gentleness, supplemented by patience.
- The remedy for avarice or greed is the virtue of generosity.
- The remedy for gluttony is the virtue of temperance.
- The remedy for lust is the virtue of chastity.

- The remedy for sloth, also known as acedia, is the virtue of diligence.

There is, of course, much more to say on practicing virtues. In the interest of space, however, I will refer you to the *Catechism of the Catholic Church*, paragraphs 1803 to 1829, for a thorough description of the human virtues, cardinal virtues, and theological virtues. The main point that I wish to make is that, just as good habits of training, rest, and nutrition will make you a better runner and lead you to the finish line, leading a virtuous life will make you a better person and lead you to the eternal reward of heaven.

Jesus as Friend and Brother

In addition to accepting Jesus as our Lord and Savior, we also need to cultivate a relationship with Jesus as our friend and brother. Jesus himself said to his disciples, "I no longer call you slaves, because a slave does not know what his master is doing. I have called you friends, because I have told you everything I have heard from my Father" (Jn 15:15). He also said, "You are my friends if you do what I command you. . . . This I command you: love one another" (Jn 15:14, 17). We all want to be loved. Jesus assures us that we will remain in his love if we follow his command to love one another.

Pope St. Paul VI, in an address he gave just days before he died on August 6, 1978, said that friendship is an occasion for developing many virtues, because it creates a "harmony of feelings and tastes that are quite distinct from self-love; rather it develops the dedication of one friend to the other, to very high levels—even that of heroism. . . . It [friendship] both requires and develops generosity, selflessness, sympathy, solidarity, and, especially, the possibility of making mutual sacrifices." The book of Sirach describes the great rewards of friendship:

Faithful friends are a sturdy shelter;
whoever finds one finds a treasure.
Faithful friends are beyond price,
no amount can balance their worth.
Faithful friends are life-saving medicine;
those who fear God will find them. (6:14–16)

St. Thomas Aquinas wrote in his *Summa Theologiae* that, for there to be true friendship, a response is required; the affection and good will have to be mutual. Jesus has shown his love for us, so if we truly want to be friends with him, we must show him our love by following his commandments. There is no better way to grow in the virtues than through friendship with Jesus who teaches us through the sacrifice of the cross. Friendship with our Lord and our growth in the virtues is born and grows through prayer and is nourished through worthy reception of the sacraments.

We can also relate to Jesus as a brother. As he explained to us, we are children of the same heavenly Father. He called God by the Aramaic word for father, *Abba*. And when his disciples asked him how to pray, the first words of the prayer he taught them were "Our Father." If we have the same heavenly father as Jesus, that means that Jesus is our brother, and we should love him with brotherly love. This gives us even greater motivation to look forward to the reward of heaven, so that we can spend all eternity with Jesus our brother, in the presence of God our Father, in the unity of the Holy Spirit, of whom St. Paul wrote, "For those who are led by the Spirit of God are the children of God" (Rom 8:14).

Entering the Gates of Heaven

Scripture often describes our entrance to heaven as through a gate. More clearly, Jesus said that he *is* the gate to salvation:

> Amen, amen, I say to you, I am the gate for the
> sheep. All who came [before me] are thieves and
> robbers, but the sheep did not listen to them. I am
> the gate. Whoever enters through me will be saved,
> and will come in and go out and find pasture. (Jn
> 10:7–9)

Clearly, we can't enter the gates of heaven without Jesus. While
on earth, it is necessary to cultivate our relationship with him
as Lord and Savior, friend and brother. One way to do that
is to practice the virtues. Another way for us to stay close to
Jesus is to stay close to his mother, the Blessed Virgin Mary.

Mary will lead us to her Son right up to the moment of our
death. To illustrate her role, I'd like to share something that happened to me when I was catching a flight to celebrate an out-of-
town wedding for a friend of mine. I had gift-wrapped a figurine
of the Blessed Mother as a wedding present for the newlyweds
and put the gift in my carry-on bag. When I got to the airport and
put my bag on the conveyer belt for security screening, the TSA
agent looked at the X-ray and called out, "Bag check." I immediately realized the problem: the figurine was made of leaded
crystal and the security agent must have thought it was some
sort of weapon. The TSA supervisor came over, saw me standing
there wearing my clerical suit and Roman collar, then looked
at the X-ray image of the figurine and exclaimed, "For heaven's
sake, it's the Blessed Mother! Let him through!" Of course, I was
greatly relieved, and while the incident still makes me laugh, I
have often thought that this is exactly the scenario I hope for
when I die. I pray that I will arrive at the gates of heaven with the
Blessed Mother at my side. Seeing me standing there with our
Lady beside me, St. Peter will exclaim, "For heaven's sake, it's the
Blessed Mother! Let him through!"

We can all hope for no better reward than that!

Quotation

"In the dust of defeat as well as the laurels of victory there is a glory to be found if one has done his best."
—Eric Liddell

Promise

I promise to lead a virtuous life, so that I can reap the rewards of spiritual and physical wellness.

Prayer

O God our Father, you sent your son Jesus to be our Lord, our Savior, our friend, and our brother. We ask for your grace to live a virtuous life, helping us to overcome the vices and snares with which the evil one seeks to entrap us, so that we may arrive safely at the gates of heaven to receive the great reward of eternal life in your kingdom. Help us to rid ourselves of every burden and sin that clings to us and persevere in running the race that lies before us, fixing our eyes on Jesus, your son, who lives and reigns with you in the unity of the Holy Spirit, one God, forever and ever. Amen.

8.

Rejoice

The integration of a sound mind in a sound body leads to the ultimate goal of eternal happiness.

"Rejoice in the Lord always. I shall say it again: rejoice!" (Phil 4:4). These words from St. Paul remind us that the life of a Christian should be a constant source of joy. In our relationship with God, he offers us the gifts of love and joy, which we must accept and return. Knowing that we may not always rejoice as we should, Paul explains:

> The Lord is near. Have no anxiety at all, but in everything, by prayer and petition, with thanksgiving, make your requests known to God. Then the peace of God that surpasses all understanding will guard your hearts and minds in Christ Jesus. Finally, brothers, whatever is true, whatever is honorable, whatever is just, whatever is pure, whatever is lovely, whatever is gracious, if there is any excellence and if there is anything worthy of praise, think about these things. Keep on doing what you have learned and received and heard and seen in

me. Then the God of peace will be with you. (Phi-
lippians 4:5–9)

It is not just a nice Christmas slogan to wish people joy
and peace. When we have the joy of the risen Lord in our
hearts, we will live with love for God and neighbor, and this
joy and love will fill our souls with an abiding peace.

The Runner's High

This book is about physical well-being as well as spiritual
well-being. So, you might be wondering, especially if you are
a nonrunner or a beginning runner, what possible joy can I
get out of potentially strenuous physical exercise like running?
Jesus brings joy to my soul, but what could possibly bring joy
to my body during a tough workout?

You may have heard someone mention a "runner's high,"
but may have never known what it meant. A runner's high is
not a made-up piece of lore told by those of us who run, but
a scientifically proven physical phenomenon experienced by
runners. K. Aleisha Fetters, a Chicago-based strength and
conditioning specialist, writes:

> Nature's home-brewed opiates, endorphins, are
> chemicals that act a lot like their medically engi-
> neered counterpart, morphine. Runners have cred-
> ited them for their feel-good effects for decades, but
> it wasn't until 2008 that German researchers used
> brain scans on runners and were able to identify
> exactly where they originated. The scientists found
> that during two-hour-long runs, subjects' prefron-
> tal and limbic regions (which light up in response
> to emotions like love) spewed out endorphins. The
> greater the endorphin surge in these brain areas,
> the more euphoric the runners reported feeling.

("How to Achieve a Runner's High, *Runner's World*,
December 26, 2019)

Endorphins are natural painkillers produced by your own body in response to physical discomfort. Another trigger of the runner's high has been linked to endocannabinoids, also a naturally synthesized pain reliever produced by your own body. According to Dr. Matthew Hill, associate professor at the University of Calgary's Hotchkiss Brain Institute, the most examined endocannabinoid produced in the body, anandamide, is believed to create a feeling of calmness. He explains that endorphins can be created only by specialized neurons, but almost any cell in the body is capable of making endocannabinoids, which means they have the potential to make a bigger impact on your brain.

> In a summary of the research of German scientists, Judy Lavelle described how researchers have shown the brain's endocannabinoid system may also play a role in producing a runner's high: "The researchers hit upon the endocannabinoid system as possibly being involved because they observed that endorphins can't pass through the blood-brain barrier. On the other hand, a lipid-soluble endocannabinoid called anandamide—also found at high levels in people's blood after running—can travel from the blood into the brain, where it can trigger a high" ("New Brain Effects behind Runner's High," *Chemical and Engineering News*, 2015).

Additionally, several studies have emphasized the fact that people need eight hours of sleep a night for optimal endocannabinoid production (see chapter 6). Moreover, research shows that endocannabinoid levels are three times greater first thing in the morning compared with late at night before going to bed. Perhaps that is why my running in the morning wakes me up and makes me feel so refreshed.

Laughing at the Finish Line

Have I ever experienced the runner's high? Absolutely, yes! Usually I don't experience a runner's high *while* I am running, but almost always *after* a long training run, and especially at the end of a marathon. It's not just a matter of feeling relieved that the long run is over, but there is definitely a chemical reaction going on in my brain that gives me a heightened sense of euphoria.

Almost every photo taken of me crossing the finish line shows me with a big smile on my face. In fact, people who have met me at the finish have said, "You look pretty good for having just run 26.2 miles!" In fact, during the final stretch of a marathon I ran with my friend Bryan Gilpin, I started laughing out loud when we reached the final stretch. And this wasn't just some muffled chuckling, but loud guffaws! Bryan looked at me and asked, "What's so funny?" I laughed again, pointed ahead, and exclaimed, "It's the finish line!" As they say, I guess you had to be there.

Seeing the finish line after running twenty-six miles and knowing that there are only two-tenths of a mile left to run is certainly cause for rejoicing. I am not usually a highly emotional person, but at the end of a marathon I usually am laughing or crying or both! I think these kinds of outbursts are effects of runner's high. A similar thing happens on a long training run. I can feel the endorphins and endocannabinoids flying through my brain. If that makes running an addiction, at least it's a healthy one!

Playing for Fun

I believe that all sports should be a time for rejoicing. Sports should bring you fun and bring you joy at all times, not just

over the course of a runner's high. One of the obstacles to
playing for fun is the fact that so many children are channeled
into organized sports and competitive leagues at an early age.
As a boy, I would go with my brothers and our friends from
the neighborhood to "The Boulevard," a parkway of green
grass along Marshall Boulevard in Chicago, which was only a
block away from our house. My family lived in an apartment
above our family pharmacy, and there was neither a front
yard nor a back yard, so "The Boulevard" was the closest open
space to play. There was no baseball diamond, so we would
just designate natural objects like trees as first base, second
base, and third base. It didn't matter if they were not exactly
ninety feet apart. It worked for us.

We also played floor hockey in the basement below the
pharmacy, calling our makeshift hockey arena the "Cermak
Coliseum," since our apartment building was on Cermak
Road. Our contrived baseball parks and hockey rinks could
become whatever major league venue we wanted to imagine in
our minds, and we could be any big-league pitcher or hockey
player to suit our fantasies. I could be Tommy John pitching
on the mound (even if I did throw right-handed and he threw
lefty) or Glenn Hall playing goalie in the nets for the Blackhawks. Winning and losing were important to us, but what
loomed larger in our minds was the fun of playing what we
wanted to play in the way that we wanted to play. After all, the
meanings of play and fun are nearly identical.

My philosophy of fun and sports was put to the test
a few years ago when I was coaching the goalies for the
hockey team at Sacred Heart-Griffin Catholic High School
in Springfield. Actually, in most of the years that I have
been helping to coach the SHG hockey team, we have had
only one goalie. This was the case when Keith Steele was
our goalie. What made it even more interesting is that
Keith was only a freshman. Now goaltending is one of the

most stressful positions in all of sports. Most players in other positions can make a mistake and often it will not be that big a deal or may not even be noticed, but when a goalie makes a mistake and allows a goal, everyone in the rink knows it. That's a lot of pressure, especially for a high school freshman.

We won our first game of the season eight to six, but I could tell Keith was not happy about giving up six goals. When we lost our next game, Keith was even more upset, blaming himself for the loss. Our third game was on the big ice surface at the University of Illinois in Champaign-Urbana. I could imagine the pressure building on Keith. After our warmups on the ice and just before the puck was dropped to start the game, the team would gather near the bench to hear last minute instructions by our coach. But the goalie would come over to me as his goalie coach for some last-minute tips before starting the game.

So when Keith skated over to me, I simply asked him, "Keith, why do you play this game? What is your objective?"

He thought briefly and answered, "To win."

I said, "No, that shouldn't be your main objective. Don't get me wrong. I am very competitive. I love to win and I hate to lose, but the most important objective of this game is to have fun. I don't want you to get so upset with yourself every time you give up a goal or lose a game that you will wind up hating hockey and quit playing when you graduate high school. I'm still playing hockey because I have fun when I play. I want you to enjoy this game so much that you'll still be playing when you're my age. So just go out there and have fun!"

With that, Keith got a big smile on his face, skated out to his net, and played a great game. I think a big reason why he played a great game was that he was more relaxed and looser, instead of stressed out and uptight. Keith was having fun with every save he made. By the way, we won that game too!

The Beatitudes: Jesus' Formula for Happiness and Joy

In the summer of 2005 I made my first trip to the Holy Land. I had been part of a Catholic-Jewish dialogue group for a few years in Chicago when some of us from the group decided to make a pilgrimage together. So a bishop, three priests and two rabbis went to the Holy Land. Sounds like the start of a bad joke, right? It was no joke and there is no punchline. We indeed set out for our pilgrimage to the land held sacred by Christians, Jews, and Muslims.

Since our rabbi friends had been to Israel several times previously, they coordinated the trip. They were aware of the places that Catholic priests would be interested in seeing. When we arrived in Tel Aviv after an overnight flight, we hit the ground running. We immediately travelled by bus to Galilee as our bodies tried to acclimate to the local time zone. When we arrived, it was daytime and warm. The rabbis had arranged for me and the priests to celebrate the holy Mass at an outdoor altar at the Mount of the Beatitudes, where Jesus gave his Sermon on the Mount that is recorded in chapter 5 of the Gospel of Matthew.

I had often heard it said that you will never read the Bible quite the same way after visiting the Holy Land in person. This occasion in Galilee showed me that this was certainly true.

The very title "Sermon on the Mount" always suggested in my mind a scene of Jesus standing on a mountain or hill as he preached. Indeed, the Mount of Beatitudes is a hill in northern Israel, in the Korazim Plateau. What I did not know until I saw it in person is that the Mount of the Beatitudes overlooks the Sea of Galilee. As I celebrated Mass at in the fresh, warm air, I was gazing out at a magnificent scene of the sun glistening on the peaceful waters of the Sea of Galilee. I thought to myself, "No wonder Jesus picked this spot for his Sermon on the Mount: the view is breathtaking!"

Each one of the Beatitudes starts out with the word translated as "blessed," which comes from the Greek word *makarios*, which some Bibles translate as "happy." When St. Jerome translated the Bible into Latin, he translated the Greek word *makarios* as *beati* in Latin, from which we get the noun "beatitude," which refers to a state of great joy. Indeed, if you are very happy, you might describe this feeling as beatitude. Also in this way, Catholic theology speaks of the "beatific vision," that is, the blessed or happy sight of seeing God's face in heaven.

Notice that Jesus concludes the Beatitudes by proclaiming, "Rejoice and be glad, for your reward will be great in heaven." Indeed, the beatific vision, seeing God's face in heaven, is a great reward that will bring unsurpassed gladness and joy.

Arête as the Key to Happiness

In chapter 7, we discussed the virtues, that is, living according to good habits. There is a connection between virtuous living and being happy. The Greek philosopher Aristotle wrote in his *Nicomachean Ethics* that happiness is "an activity of the soul in accordance with virtue." He added that a person "is happy who lives in accordance with complete virtue." By "complete virtue," Aristotle is saying that it is not enough to have a few virtues, as if you could just pick out the ones you like and forget the rest, like going through the buffet line at a cafeteria; rather, one must strive to possess all of the virtues.

Learning about the virtuous life was one of the hallmarks of my high school education. It's hard for me to believe, but May 29, 2020 marked fifty years since I graduated from high school seminary. We received a classical education, which included four years of Latin, Greek and Roman mythology, English literature, history, music, math, science, and, of course, religion. One of the worst insults we would use back then against a classmate was to call him a "Philistine." This name, which described a "non-Israelite" in the Bible, meant in this case someone who was hostile or indifferent to culture and the arts, or who had no understanding of them. Yes, times have changed even in how we insult someone!

In contrast to the derogatory insult, "Philistine," a very positive term that we learned in high school was the Greek term *arête*, which expresses the idea of being the best that one can possibly be—in a word: *excellence*. We are called to strive for *arête* in every aspect of our lives through the practice of the virtues. Greek literature provides us with excellent examples of how to do this. In *"Arête: The Greek Idea of Excellence,"* S. Snyder writes:

> In the *Iliad*, an epic tale emerging from the distant Greek past, it is a term associated with warriors who exemplify bravery, fierceness and physical skill. Characters like Achilles or Hector represent a nearly perfect realization of humanity in a warlike, tribal society.
>
> In *The Odyssey*, a slightly later epic, *arête* is used to describe Odysseus, who combines the warrior-hero's courage with wit, cunning and resourcefulness. *Arête* is also used to describe Odysseus's wife, Penelope, who demonstrates that even misfortune and sorrow can be suffered with excellence.
>
> And lastly, the Greeks provide us with still another manifestation of *arête*: Socrates, a very new and different kind of Greek hero. Socrates was a real person, a Fifth Century BCE Athenian who

has come to symbolize for us the life dedicated to
the pursuit of moral and intellectual excellence.

Although the Greek notion of *arête* precedes Christianity, we can also say that *arête* pertains to the vocation of all Christians. The goal of Christianity is not excellence in and of itself, but salvation. While we Christians do not seek excellence for its own sake, we are called to excellence in striving for holiness, so that we can reap the fruits of the salvation that Christ has won for us.

St. Augustine, who served as a bishop in North Africa in the fifth century and who is one of the greatest theologians of all time, wrote that true happiness will come only in eternal life: "Rejoice in the Lord, not in the world. That is, rejoice in the truth, not in wickedness; rejoice in the hope of eternity, not in the fading flower of vanity. That is the way to rejoice."

Joyful Living through Stewardship and Service

In chapter 7, I wrote that being a disciple of our Lord means putting Christ at the center of our lives, in the very depths of our hearts, and living in such a way that reflects the fact that Jesus is our sovereign Master. Stewardship flows from our discipleship. Stewardship is our joyful and generous response in gratitude to God for the gifts of his creation.

Some people mistakenly think that stewardship is only about offering a financial contribution. There is indeed a financial aspect to it in terms of seeing ourselves as stewards of God's creation, but stewardship is more than giving money; it is about the giving of our entire selves. God created everything and so it must be said that everything belongs to him. We are merely caretakers of God's creation that he has generously shared with us. When we recognize this, we can rejoice at having been the fortunate recipients of God's generosity and respond in kind by sharing these gifts with those in need. When people talk about "giving back" to the community, they are basically talking about practicing stewardship. This applies to "giving back" to the running community you become a part of when you take up running.

One of the benefits of joining the Chicago Area Runners Association was not only having a pace group to run with, but also having a group leader who shared her wisdom from her previous years of marathon running. So after a couple of years as a member of the group, I decided to give back to the running community by volunteering as a group leader myself. The fact that I run at a pretty consistent pace was a big help. The members of my pace group called me a "human metronome" because the pace I set was so regular and consistent, like when my brother Allen and I set out to run our first Chicago Marathon at a ten-minute pace and finished with an overall average of 10:01 per mile.

After running the Chicago Marathon seven times, I decided to run marathons in some other cities. Because the marathons I chose were often on weekends other than the Chicago Marathon, I volunteered when Chicago Marathon officials were looking for help managing the growing crowds at the start line. Also, when I first started running the Chicago Marathon in 1995, there were fewer than 9,000 finishers. Ten years later, that number had more than tripled to 32,995. That year, 2005, was also my last Chicago Marathon, as it had become so crowded that getting to the start line was a real challenge because of pedestrian gridlock. So the following year, when Chicago Marathon officials put out the call for volunteers to help manage the flow at the start line, I volunteered since I knew from first-hand experience what the problem was and was willing to help people get where they needed to be for the start of the marathon. For as much as I had enjoyed being a participant in previous marathons, it was also a joy to serve as a race volunteer to help make the marathon a happy experience for other runners as well.

Virtuous Living through Vocation

Responding to the call to serve is what we call a vocation. The word *vocation* comes from the Latin word *vocare*, which means "to call." A vocation is what God calls us to do with our lives. For most, a person's specific vocation is to marriage and family life. For some, God's call comes in the form of a vocation to priesthood or consecrated life as a religious sister or brother. A vocation is the fullest expression of stewardship, for it entails giving of your entire self, either to your spouse in the Sacrament of Matrimony or to the Church in the Sacrament of Holy Orders or the profession of vows as a consecrated religious.

In addition to the concept of a vocation in the larger sense of God's call to marriage, family life, the priesthood, or consecrated life, we can also understand vocation in the more ordinary sense of what God is calling us to do each day in the little details of our life. Both our overall vocation to the Christian life and our specific vocations within the Church involve *arête*, the call to excellence through our everyday actions. St. Josemaría Escrivá is considered to be the saint of everyday holiness. Pope St. John Paul II called St. Josemaría "the saint of ordinary life" for his message that holiness and sainthood are attainable by all the faithful in our everyday lives at work and school, and within our families; indeed wherever we find ourselves.

I think it is fair to say that running is a form of vocation that fits the overall meaning of the term. Running certainly involves a quest for excellence, typically improvement on times and distance goals. Running has been a major part of my life and I have spent many hours running for over fifty years, so somehow this must be part of God's plan and call for me.

So you should ask yourself: do you have a vocation to be a runner? Put differently: if you have never run before, is God calling you now to be a runner? If you are a runner, but have never run a marathon, might God be calling you to run a marathon?

Asking those questions may seem easier than trying to answer them. You may be wondering: How am I supposed to know what God wants me to do with my life, let alone whether he wants me to run? That's a good question. I try to answer it by telling people that God speaks to us in a variety of ways: God speaks to us in the Bible, which indeed we call the Word of God; God speaks to us in prayer, which by definition is conversation with God; and God speaks to us in our hearts, which we can discern through meditation and contemplation, as I described earlier in this book.

There is yet another way that God speaks to us, a way that is often overlooked: God speaks to us through other people. In my own experience as well as in talking to many other priests, seminarians, and women religious, our religious vocations often came because somebody, even a stranger, said to a young man: "You should think about being a priest. I think you would be a good priest." Or to a young woman: "You should think about being a religious sister. I think you would make a wonderful nun."

I believe that God speaks to people in the context of marriage as well. Think about it. When someone asks, "Will you marry me?" might that not be God speaking through that person? After all, the Bible says that "God is love" (1 Jn 4:8), so if someone is moved by love to propose marriage, is that not a sign that God has touched that person's heart and prompted this expression of love?

God also speaks to us in various ways in the less profound and more ordinary matters of everyday life. I became a runner because I read about the cardiovascular benefits of aerobic training when I was a teenager worried about my genetic disposition to heart disease. I became a marathon runner because I repeatedly heard people who knew that I was a runner asking me if I was ever going to run a marathon. Maybe reading this book will inspire you to start running or even run a marathon! Perhaps if you have fallen away from the practice of the faith, reading this book may be God's way of calling you back to Church. The prophet Hosea proclaimed strongly, "Return to the Lord, your God" (Hos 14:2). Maybe his words are being spoken right now directly to you.

Mary, Cause of Our Joy

Why are we so joyful? I think a case can be made around the announcement of the birth of Jesus—the Annunciation—as the cause of our great joy.

I have now been to the Holy Land a total of three times. Each time that I have visited the Church of the Annunciation in Nazareth, built on the site where, according to the Gospel of Luke, the archangel Gabriel appeared to Mary to announce that "you will conceive in your womb and bear a son, and you shall name him Jesus." This message puzzled Mary, so she asked the angel, "How can this be, since I have no relations with a man?" The angel said to her in reply, "The Holy Spirit will come upon you, and the power of the Most High will overshadow you. Therefore the child to be born will be called holy, the Son of God . . . for nothing will be impossible for God." Mary said, "Behold, I am the handmaid of the Lord. May it be done to me according to your word" (Lk 1:31–38). Mary's affirmative response is known as the *fiat*, Latin for "may it be done." It may be said that the history of the human race hinged on this unique divine event which gives meaning to our existence.

There is an inscription at the base of the altar in the lower level crypt of the Church of the Annunciation in Nazareth that says in Latin *Verbum Caro Hic Factum Est*, which means "The Word was made flesh here." It is the word *hic* ("here") that makes this inscription unique. Only in Nazareth can this *hic* be said. Elsewhere in the world we say in the Creed, *Verbum Caro Factum Est*, which means "The Word was made flesh." Adding this short word *hic* to this article of our faith adds to the power of this statement, for it proclaims, "Here, right here!" is where God took on our human nature in the flesh, not just in some abstract sense, but as a theological statement. This is the cause of our joy.

Pope St. Paul VI, in his 1975 Apostolic Exhortation *Gaudete in Domino* (Rejoice in the Lord), invites us to think about how Mary rejoiced at her Son's Resurrection. She is "unreservedly open to the joy of the resurrection. . . . She recapitulates all joys, lives the perfect joy promised to the Church: *Mater plena sanctae laetitiae* [Mother full of holy joy] she is, and with every reason her children on earth, turning their eyes toward the Mother of hope and the Mother of grace, invoke her as the Cause of their Joy—*causa nostrae laetitiae*."

Be joyful in your quest for spiritual and physical wellness. Proclaim your joy often with this hymn to Mary sung during the Easter season that proclaims the joy of the Resurrection:

> Queen of heaven, rejoice, alleluia.
> The Son whom you merited to bear, alleluia,
> has risen as he said, alleluia.
> Pray for us to God, alleluia.
> Rejoice and be glad, O Virgin Mary, alleluia!
> For the Lord has truly risen, alleluia!

Quotation

"Let Mary's soul be in each of you to proclaim the greatness of the Lord."

—St. Ambrose

Promise

I promise to make something beautiful for God as I run for a higher purpose, striving for spiritual and physical wellness.

Prayer

O God, give us the grace of spiritual and physical wellness, and in your compassion hear our prayers, that, rejoicing in our Lord's Resurrection, we may merit to receive the joy of our redemption. Through our Lord Jesus Christ, your Son, who lives and reigns with you in the unity of the Holy Spirit, one God, for ever and ever. Amen.

Epilogue

Let's take a moment—and one more "r"—to *recap* the eight steps of running for a higher purpose on the path to spiritual and physical fitness that we covered in this book:

1. Review: making an honest assessment of our situation and our need to improve
2. Reform: identifying how to improve
3. Resolve: determining how to put those steps toward improvement into effect
4. Repeat: continuing our efforts lest we quit before seeing any real improvement
5. Renew: bringing about a renewal of physical and spiritual wellness
6. Relax: balancing effort with rest to prevent burnout
7. Reward: achieving the satisfaction of physical and spiritual wellness
8. Rejoice: celebrating the joy of eternal happiness

Some of the means I described in terms of running for a higher purpose involve having the proper motivation, using a tried and tested training program, drawing strength from running buddies and mentors, praying while running, and raising money for charitable causes. I also discussed many of the treasures of our Catholic tradition, such as praying the Rosary, following the Ten Commandments, aspiring to the virtues while avoiding vices, and living the Beatitudes as a path to happiness here on earth and for all eternity.

I purposely did not make a hard distinction between the spiritual and physical aspects that I addressed in this book because we are not dualistic beings, as if our bodies and souls were separated from each other. Each person's body and soul are holistic elements of one integrated reality, namely, the total person that you are. Thus, I did not write one chapter about running techniques and the next about spiritual matters, as if they were distinct and unrelated elements, but wove them together throughout this book. The point is that if our bodies are ill, our souls will be dispirited, and if our spirits are down, our bodies will be adversely affected. Conversely, good physical health helps us to feel good and enhances our mental acuity, while being at peace in our souls will contribute to our physical well-being.

Most Rev. Thomas J. Paprocki is the bishop of Springfield. A Chicago native, he was ordained a priest of the Archdiocese of Chicago in 1978. He served as auxiliary bishop of Chicago from 2003 to 2010.

After ordination, Paprocki studied law at DePaul University and was admitted to the Illinois bar in 1981. He cofounded the South Chicago Legal Clinic to help the poor with legal services. In 2014, he was named president and of-counsel for the organization, which is now called the Greater Chicago Legal Clinic. Paprocki completed his doctorate at the Pontifical Gregorian University in Rome in 1991 and his MBA from the University of Notre Dame in 2013. He served in a variety of pastoral and administrative roles in the Archdiocese of Chicago. He was an adjunct professor of law at Loyola University Chicago from 1999 to 2015 and has served in the same capacity at Notre Dame since 2016.

The connection between sports and faith is a focus of Paprocki's ministry. He is an avid hockey player and runner, having run twenty-four marathons throughout the world and raised about $500,000 for charity. Paprocki is the chairman of the Episcopal Advisory Board of Catholic Athletes for Christ. He is the author of *Holy Goals for Body and Soul: Eight Steps to Connect Sports with God and Faith.*